Understanding Human Communication

Understanding Human Communication

Why Communication Is Important and How to Be Good at It

First Edition

Edited by Timothy R. Levine and Samantha J. Shebib

University of Oklahoma
University of Alabama at Birmingham

cognella®

SAN DIEGO

Bassim Hamadeh, CEO and Publisher
Angela Schultz, Senior Field Acquisitions Editor
Craig Lincoln, Project Editor
Susana Christie, Senior Developmental Editor
Rachel Kahn, Production Editor
Emely Villavicencio, Senior Graphic Designer
Laura Duncan, Licensing Coordinator
Natalie Piccotti, Director of Marketing
Kassie Graves, Senior Vice President, Editorial
Alia Bales, Director, Project Editorial and Production

Contents

Forward   vii

Unit I   The Centrality of Communication   1

Chapter 1   The Importance of Social Integration   3
Chapter 2   Communication Is a Process   9
Chapter 3   Meme State Activation   15
Chapter 4   Three Types of Questions   21
Chapter 5   Five Perspectives on Human Communication   27

Unit II   Communication and Influence   33

Chapter 6   Sound and Strong Argument   35
Chapter 7   Evidence   41
Chapter 8   Source Credibility   45
Chapter 9   Emotional Appeals   49
Chapter 10   Cialdini's Weapons of Influence   53
Chapter 11   Compliance-Gaining Strategies   59
Chapter 12   The Audience   65
Chapter 13   Diffusion of Innovations   69

Unit III   Being Better Communicators   73

Chapter 14   Nonverbal Communication   75
Chapter 15   Culture and Communication   85

Chapter 16   Sex, Gender, and Beyond the Binary   **89**

Chapter 17   Goffman and Self-Presentation   **95**

Chapter 18   Uncertainty and Attributions   **101**

Chapter 19   Fairness and Equity   **107**

Chapter 20   Theory of Mind and Empathy   **111**

Chapter 21   Networks   **115**

Chapter 22   Personality   **119**

Chapter 23   Family Communication   **125**

Chapter 24   Conflict   **131**

Chapter 25   Deception   **137**

Chapter 26   Communication Competence   **143**

References   **147**

Forward

Welcome to *Understanding Human Communication*! Our book is a bit different from most textbooks. We thought that a bit of explanation might be helpful. This book was created for CMST 105 *Introduction to Human Communication* at the University of Alabama at Birmingham (UAB). CMST 105, in its current incarnation, was created by the two of us: Professor Levine and Professor Shebib. We hope our approach is contagious and the book is used around the country and even around the world.

Our book provides an overview of human communication. For communication majors, it provides a first look at the field. Many chapters offer brief introductions to topics about which students can take whole classes. For most students, however, this may be the only communication class in their college careers.

At UAB, CMST 105 is part of the university's general education requirements. We see competent communication as an essential aspect of being an educated person. Consequently, the primary focus is on how to understand communication and how to become a better communicator. No background knowledge is required or presumed. This book should be accessible to all.

Several features set our book apart from most other college textbooks. First, each chapter is written in one of our voices and begins with a first-person narrative. We chose this format for many reasons. Our style is engaging and less dry than more typical texts. It helps personalize the content. The stories have a point and exemplify content.

Pay attention when the voice changes. Not all chapters are in the same voice. Not all the stories are being told by the same person. Be aware of whose voice you are reading.

We introduce ourselves here because, as we said, the chapters are written in one or the other of our voices. Hopefully this way the narratives make more sense from the start. In the language of communication, we are seeking to provide context.

Levine here: I wrote the first several chapters. I am a balding white guy who has been a communication professor for a long time. By communication professor standards, I am very successful and accomplished. I am married and my wife is also a very successful and accomplished professor of communication. I have lived all over. I grew up in Arizona, and have taught college in West Virginia, Michigan, Indiana, Hawaii, South Korea, and Alabama. I went to graduate school in communication because I was interested in persuasion. Along the way, I became best known for my research on deception and for Truth-Default Theory. The author Malcolm Gladwell popularized my work in his book *Talking to Strangers*. I have another book titled *Duped* that is about deception. Besides teaching and writing, I like to cook. I consider myself a foodie and I like food too much for my own good. I am a sushi snob, especially regarding uni. As for music, these days I listen to the Grateful Dead, Phish, and Frank

Zappa. There will be more about me throughout the book. But next, I will let Professor Shebib introduce herself to you all as we switch to her voice.

Shebib here: Dr. Levine brought me into this textbook when I first started as an assistant professor at UAB. I attended Arizona State University for my undergraduate degree, Illinois State University for my master's, Michigan State University for my doctorate, and did a year postdoc at Utah State University. My main research interest lies in conflict. I find the need to study conflict essential because it's inevitable and the consequences it has on personal health and relational health can be devasting if not communicated constructively and productively. Growing up my parents were very destructive and dysfunctional when handling conflict and it was very hard dealing with as a child. I mean, so much so this is what I do for a living—study conflict. Researchers have been studying conflict for decades. But what research lacks is how to change dysfunctional patterns of conflict interaction to more functional patterns. That's my overall goal—How can people change their destructive communication once it's become a habit in a relationship. My future work in conflict is interested in examining how physiological responses (i.e., cortisol and testosterone) affect how one communicates when conflict transpires. Similarly, I intend to use functional magnetic resonance imaging (fMRI) to see how conflict messages affect the brain, which is the biological organ of communication. My second area of research focuses on social support. My future work is something that is close to my heart as I've lost 9 friends in 11 years to addiction. Thus, I want to study family communication with a substance dependent family member and address communication strategies for how to support without enabling. Severe substance use and compulsive behavioral problems create significant damage to family rituals and roles. A healthy family relationship is the single biggest predictor of long-term recovery for those impacted by addiction.

The chapters are generally short and quick reads. They are to the point and cover the main ideas. We intend this brevity to encourage students to do the assigned reading. It is not a heavy lift or a big ask. Students should be able to maximize their effort-to-learning ratio. If students have to miss a class, they can get the main points from the chapter. For those attending class, each chapter primes the forthcoming lecture by providing highlights and background knowledge. After class, chapters are helpful in prioritizing the main points and serving as a reminder of course content.

Third, we are mindful that college is expensive. We sought to write an affordable book. Our book lacks the features of big, big-selling texts, but we hope it does its job well at a much lower cost.

We hope that you enjoy our book and that it is educational, informative, and engaging.

Timothy R. Levine
Samantha J. Shebib
Birmingham, Alabama, May 16, 2024

Unit I

The Centrality of Communication

CHAPTER 1

The Importance of Social Integration

[*Dr. Levine's Voice*]

I went to college at Northern Arizona University, majoring in psychology and minoring in communication. During the winter break of my junior year, I returned to my hometown of Scottsdale, Arizona, intent on relaxing, sleeping in, and watching lots of football. My father, however, was having none of my on-vacation attitude. He bluntly told me to "get a job!" I explained that I was only home for 3 weeks, and no one was going to hire me for just 3 weeks. "I'm going to quit after just three weeks" is not a winning interview strategy. Moreover, not mentioning that would be dishonest. I was quite proud of my fine argument. To my surprise, it failed. We will talk about making arguments in Chapter 6.

My Dad thought about my argument and found it reasonable. But he had an outside-the-box counter that I did not see coming. How about if he covered the cost for me to go to real estate school over break so I could get my real estate license? I could do an intensive all-day, 2-week program. I did not have a good rebuttal, so I spent my not-a-vacation-after-all in real estate school. This is an example of collaborative conflict resolution we will talk about in Chapter 25. Anyway, I was in with a bunch of attorneys and brokers from other states who needed an Arizona real estate license. Fortunately, I was a college student. I could do note-taking, studying, and test taking. Consequently, I did not find either the class or the state licensing exam especially difficult. At age 20, I was licensed to sell real estate in the state of Arizona.

The following summer, when I came home, I looked for a job as I did every summer. In the past, I had been a dishwasher, a pizza maker, a chauffeur, a busboy at various fine dining restaurants, a yard service worker, and an electrician's assistant. That summer, I interviewed for a job selling time-share condominiums. I got the job, and I made enough money in my first week to cover 3 years of my college tuition.

Just being licensed was not enough to get hired. During the interview, the manager asked me why he should hire a college kid instead of an experienced salesperson. It was a good question and one that I anticipated. My answer was that I understood people, and I understood persuasion. I knew what worked and why. "Hire me," I said, "and I will prove it."

My pay was 100% based on commission. No sales, no income. As it turned out, I really did understand people, and I understood persuasion. I was adept at convincing people to buy what I was selling. I applied what I had learned in school, and that gave me an edge over people with more experience but less understanding. Communication and people skills are important; they are valuable, and they are valued. These are the main themes of this chapter and of this book. Throughout this book, Professor Shebib and I will share what we have learned about effective communication. But we also want you to know why understanding communication is important.

Here is a quick postscript. Although I made a lot of money quickly, I hated the job. Time-shares were not right for many of the people we were selling to, and the job felt unethical. I quit after a month. Ethics and morality are important too. We will talk about questions of value in Chapter 4. It is important not to lose sight of what is right and wrong. We want to be effective communicators, but we also want to be good people. As we will see in

Chapter 26 and throughout this book, these go hand in hand. Competent communicators are not only effective in achieving their communication goals, but they also prioritize their goals well and achieve them ethically.

The Human in Human Communication

Last summer break, I started reading *Sapiens: A Brief History of Humankind* by Yuval Noh Harari.[1] It is a terrific book, and it should be required reading for all educated people. As I write this, it has 4.6 (out of 5) stars on Amazon.com with more than 30,000 ratings. It has been published for more than 2 years, and it is still in the top 10 on Amazon's rankings. Harari has a PhD in history from Oxford, and he is a professor in Israel. (I revisit this paragraph when we get to Chapters 7 and 8 on evidence and credibility. I'm using evidence to establish the credibility of the ideas I am talking about.)

Sapiens is about humans. **The *human* part of human communication is critical.** Humans communicate differently than other species, and our communication abilities have shaped who we are as a species, how we have evolved and progressed, and our individual life experiences. Understanding humankind is critical to understanding human communication, and understanding human communication is critical to understanding humankind. **This locates communication at the core of human social science.**

You all probably know that biologically speaking, we humans are *Homo sapiens*. Homo is our genus, and sapiens is our species. Currently, we sapiens are the only living humans (species belonging to the genus Homo). This was not always the case. From about 2 million to 10,000 years ago, the earth was populated with other species of humans. To list some, there were *Homo denisova, Homo erectus, Homo ergaster, Homo floresiesis, Homo neanderthalensis, Homo rudolfensis*, and *Homo soloensis*. These were separate species, not "missing links." The other human species were not our direct genetic ancestors. Rather, they were different branches of the same genetic tree.

What happened to these other variations of being human? How is it that we made it to the present day, and they did not? One possibility is that we sapiens literally killed off the competition. Once sapiens migrated to a new area, other local humans disappeared sometime thereafter. Further, endangered species due to human activity is not exclusively a recent development. Humans were hunting large mammals to extinction way back in the past. Humans show up, and then other species disappear.

What moved sapiens to the top of the food chain? We were not the strongest nor the fastest. This was long before we had guns. The things that gave us our decisive advantage were that we were good at working together in large groups and that we could pass along information and knowledge to each other. It was communication and the benefits that stemmed from communication that were critical. Communication lets us efficiently coordinate our activities and work together. It also lets us learn from each other. In our more recent history, we can even learn from people we never met. You do not have to meet me to learn from me. You can just read this book. We can pass along knowledge, and knowledge can accumulate and build on prior knowledge. This moved us from hunter-gatherers to subsistence farmers to city dwellers to scientists and industrialists to members of the information age with our cell phones, Internet, and social media.

1. Harari (2015).

The Most Important Things

Take a moment and reflect on what you think is the most important thing in life. If you were asked that question, how would you answer? How do you think other people would answer?

There is a good amount of survey research on the topic, spanning time and locations.[2] Our relationships with other people usually top the list. Family often comes out on top. Health is also near the top. Things like money, job, and religion are usually well down the list. You see similar answers if people are asked what is important to their overall happiness. A recent survey found that relationships were again the top answer, followed by health.[3]

Communication competence is key to both having high-quality relationships and good health. The link between communication and relationships is, I hope, obvious to you. Communication is how we get to know others and how we have a good relationship with others. The link between communication and health, however, may be a bit less obvious, but it is fascinating.

There are lots of ways that communication is related to health. We can do health campaigns to get people to have a healthier diet, exercise more, or practice safe sex. If you go to the doctor, you need to be able to describe your symptoms. You might take this for granted, but when I lived in Korea, I was hospitalized twice, once for food poisoning and a second time for broken bones. I do not speak Korean, so communicating with the doctors and nurses was a challenge that affected my care. Following the doctor's orders involves communication too. These examples, however, are not where I am going with this discussion of health and communication. Instead, I am going to talk about social integration and mortality. Good relationships are one secret to living a longer life, and relationships require communication.

Social Integration and Mortality

One of my many research heroes is the psychologist John Cacioppo from the University of Chicago. Among communication students and professors, Cacioppo is mostly known as one of the authors of the elaboration likelihood model (ELM) of persuasion.[4] ELM is a very influential theory of persuasion, although I am not a huge fan of it. If you take a persuasion class, you are sure to encounter it. Instead, what makes me a huge fan is Cacioppo's work on loneliness.[5]

Cacioppo's research unpacks the causal relationship between social integration and mortality in a way that is academically sophisticated, compelling, and profound. To explain this, let us start with the relationship between social integration and mortality. Social integration means being connected to other people. People with high-quality relationships with other people are socially integrated. People who are not well socially integrated feel isolated and lonely. Mortality has to do with how likely someone is to live or die. The finding is that socially integrated people have longer life expectancies than socially isolated people, and the strength of the association is stronger than you might guess. More on this in a bit.

Before continuing, we need a brief digression into the topic of meta-analyses, which is a type of evidence we will encounter several times over different topics and chapters throughout this book. **Meta-analysis is a**

---

2. For example, see Bowling (1995) and Moore (2003).

3. Schwab (2020).

4. See Petty and Cacioppo (1986b).

5. For a summary, see Cacioppo and Patrick (2008).

study of studies. In most social science research studies (let us call them primary studies), individual people are studied. In meta-analysis, each data point comes from the results of a primary study. For example, in one of the meta-analyses discussed in the next paragraph, results are cumulated across 148 primary studies with a combined sample size of over 300,000 participants. Meta-analysis gives us the big picture across lots of prior studies.

What meta-analyses of social isolation and mortality show is that lonely and socially isolated people have an increased risk of death. This was true for both objective (e.g., living alone versus living with others) and subjective (e.g., scores on a loneliness scale) assessments of social isolation, and it holds up when statistically controlling for a variety of factors such as age, socioeconomic status, and initial health status.[6] What I find especially stunning is how social isolation compares to other things that adversely affect mortality. The effect of social isolation is about as bad as smoking more than 15 cigarettes per day, and it is a larger risk factor than obesity![7] I was amazed when I read this.

Cacioppo's research was a massive multidisciplinary deep dive into why loneliness and social isolation are so bad for us. Here is the condensed version of what he found.[8] Social integration gives us comfort and security, while social isolation puts us on edge. When we feel isolated, we become more wary of our fellow humans, and we are more likely to take offense and read bad motives into other's actions. This takes a toll on us over time, and it interferes with our sleep. Little sounds wake us up. Chronic poor sleep affects our hormonal system, which, in turn, over time, reduces the effectiveness of our immune system. Impaired immune responses make it easier to get sick and harder to recover once we are sick. Social isolation starts a chain reaction that increases our risk of death by changing how we perceive others, harming our sleep, and ultimately impairing immunity. Avoiding social isolation and being socially integrated necessarily involves communication. Having good relations with others enacted through high-quality, competent communication is good for our health.

Jobs Matter Too

In the greater scheme of things, your job may not rival the importance of personal relationships, health, and social integration. This said, jobs matter too. As a department chair at University of Alabama at Birmingham (UAB), I meet with families on college recruitment campus visits. I learned quickly that the number one most frequently asked question was about internship possibilities. Jobs were on the students' and their parents' minds when thinking about which college to attend. I am a strong believer that being educated is not just job training, and the value of an education is not only a future salary return on the time and tuition investment. This said, understanding communication is job relevant, and it is another reason that understanding communication is important.

Research consistently finds that communication skills (oral, written, interpersonal, teamwork) are highly valued by employers.[9] Similarly, research shows that communication skills are also an important consideration in who gets promoted.[10]

For example, when I was a young professor in Hawaii, I led a collaboration between Hawaiian Electric

---

6. Holt-Lunstad et al. (2015).

7. Holt-Lunstad and Smith (2010).

8. Cacioppo and Patrick (2008).

9. For example, see Baird and Parayitam (2019) and NACE (2020).

10. Reinsch and Gardner (2014).

(the electric utility for the islands) and the University of Hawaii. Hawaiian Electric was happy with the technical abilities of University of Hawaii engineering graduates. However, as young electrical engineers moved up from entry-level positions into management, the communication demands of their jobs increased. We designed a strategy to work more communication education into engineering classes to meet this need. Hawaiian Electric was happy to fund this effort because they understood the importance of employing people with competent communication skills.

Chapter Summary

The fictional Mr. Spock from the TV show *Star Trek* would tell people to "live long and prosper." If you think about it, that is a nice wish for others. I wish that for you. This chapter supplied a first peak at the role of communication in living a long and prosperous life. The chapter core ideas in the chapter are as follows:

- Communication is important for us humans.
- It is in our interest to understand communication and be good at it.
- Learning more about communication will help you improve your communication and thereby accrue the many benefits.
- There are three important things communication does for us.
  - Communication lets us coordinate with other humans to accomplish things we cannot do by ourselves.
  - Communication lets us learn from others, share our knowledge, and build our individual and collective knowledge bases.
  - Communication enables relationships with other humans.

In the next two chapters, we get into the details of what communication is and how we do it.

CHAPTER 2

Communication Is a Process

[Dr. Levine's Voice]

As I neared graduation from Northern Arizona University, I considered going on to graduate school. A career selling real estate was not for me. I chose communication over psychology for several reasons. Obtaining a graduate teaching assistantship, waiving tuition, and paying a monthly stipend was, and still is, easier in communication.[1] Many of my favorite classes (persuasion, presidential campaign rhetoric, and nonverbal communication) were communication classes. Perhaps the decisive sequence of events, however, was that during my senior year, my favorite professor, Dr. Harold Larson, organized a university-sponsored road trip to attend the Western Communication Association conference in Fresno, California. At that conference, I met two famous communication professors: Dr. Michael J. Beatty and Dr. James C. McCroskey. They recruited me to grad school. Beatty and I are now long-time friends, and we have coauthored several research projects together.[2] My first article in a top communication journal was coauthored with Jim McCroskey.[3] Meeting them worked out well for me. This highlights the importance of communication networks (see Chapter 21).

At the time, Jim McCroskey was the chair of the Department of Communication Studies at West Virginia University (WVU). I had read his research on evidence and source credibility because of my interest in persuasion (see Chapters 7 and 8). Later in his career, he transitioned into studying communication apprehension and other communication traits (see Chapter 22). Analyses of prolific authorship usually list James C. McCroskey as the most published communication scholar of all time.[4,5] Michael Beatty is usually in the top five.

Anyway, shortly after I returned from the conference, I got a phone call from Dr. McCroskey, who accepted me into the master's program at WVU with full funding. I accepted on the spot.[6] After getting my master's degree from WVU's intensive 9-month program, I moved on to the highly rated and historically prominent PhD program

---

1. Most communication departments offer a multisection public speaking course that enrolls large numbers of students. These sections are often taught by graduate teaching assistants with faculty supervision. Staffing public speaking classes ensures many opportunities to fund graduate students, even at the MA level. This makes the supply-demand ratio for graduate student funding in communication favorable relative to most other academic fields.

2. For example, see Beatty et al. (2002), Duff et al. (2007), and Levine et al. (2012).

3. Levine and McCroskey (1990).

4. If a wide net is cast, I guess that Jim McCroskey, Howie Giles, and Judee Burgoon are the top three. If the narrower criteria of publications specifically in communication journals is used, I guess that Bill Benoit and I rank second and third well behind McCroskey, but ahead of people who publish more outside the field.

5. For example, see Bolkan et al. (2012).

6. Sadly, Jim is no longer with us. He ended his career at UAB, although we did not overlap. If we did, I would have been his boss. Jim and I became longtime friends and conference buddies. If you are interested, Hee Sun Park and I published this remembrance of Jim: Levine and Park (2017). You can see Jim's bio and bibliography at http://www.jamescmccroskey.com.

at Michigan State University (MSU), which, at the time, was the place to be for students interested in persuasion. Professors and graduates of MSU loom large in this and other chapters throughout this book.

Jim McCroskey authored something like 55 books on communication. That is an enormous number of books to write. In these books, he usually defined communication (I'm paraphrasing a bit) as *a process in which people stimulate meaning in the minds of others through verbal and nonverbal messages*. This is far from the only definition of communication. Different books will provide different definitions. McCroskey's definition works well for our purpose. First off, **his definition specifies that communication is a *process***. Much of the rest of this chapter will unpack that idea. Beyond that, **communication involves stimulating meaning in the minds of others**. There will be much more of this in the next chapter. Finally, we do this through *messages*. Messages will be a recurring topic throughout the book. Many communication professors see the study of messages as the defining aspect of the field. We will cover nonverbal messages in Chapter 14. Verbal aspects of messages are covered throughout this book. Just as one example, argument structure is covered in Chapter 6.

The idea that communication is a process is usually attributed to David K. Berlo, who was the founding chair of the Department of Communication at MSU, where I did my PhD Berlo authored a book in 1960 titled *The Process of Communication*, making the case that communication must be understood as a process. It would be hard to overstate the impact of Berlo's book and the ideas therein. The rest of this chapter is devoted to Berlo's depiction of communication as a process and his Source, Message, Channel, Receiver (SMCR) model of communication.

The Process Orientation to Communication

According to Berlo, understanding communication as a process involves accepting two connected premises. First, **communication is "dynamic, ongoing, ever-changing, continuous."**[7] There is fluidity and motion to communication. It transpires over time. As an analogy, I can take both still images and movies with the camera on my cell phone. Berlo's first point is that communication is more like a movie than a still image.

Second, **the components of the communication process all interact**. Each part or aspect affects the other parts. We can call this idea *interdependence*. **The people who are communicating are interdependent.** What one is doing affects the other and vice versa. Further, it is not just the people who are interdependent. **The people, the messages, the context, the media or channel(s), and the time are all interconnected and interrelated.**

Let us take your reading of this book as an example of communication. Obviously, the act of reading and the understanding you take away from reading is something that occurs over time. The specific word you might be reading at this instant does not convey the meaning of the sentence, paragraph, or chapter. The mental snapshot of what is in your head at this instant does not remotely capture what is going on any more than the word you are reading at this instant in the flow of time. Moreover, what you read later might reshape how you come to understand this sentence. What is on the page is shaped by who I am as an author. Another author would not cover the same ideas in just the same way. My understanding is not just based on the words Berlo wrote in his book. I learned about communication as a process from people like Jim McCroskey and Gerald Miller,[8] who worked with

---

7. Berlo (1960, p. 24).

8. Gerald R. Miller (1931–1993; Jerry or G. R. to his many students) was the chair of the communication department at MSU while I studied there in the late 1980s. He was an early and influential theorist and researcher on the topics of interpersonal communication, persuasion, and deception. Chapter 4 comes from Miller.

Berlo. Berlo stories were still told at MSU when I was a student there. Similarly, no two readers will take away the same things from my words here. You bring your own experience and your own perspective. Even though the words are the same, no two readings will be identical. Even things like the time of day might affect how this communication event unfolds and what future impact it might have.

The idea that communication is a process becomes even more striking when we begin to think about synchronous communication, where there is mutual, real-time back-and-forth. A gaming example may be useful. Some games are turn-based. I move, then you move, and so on. Other games are played in real time; all the players are moving and react to each other simultaneously. Both are processes. Both are dynamic, both transpire over time, and both involve interdependence. Early moves shape later moves. Other players' moves affect our moves and vice versa. But the process of the game is different, and in synchronous, real-time games, the process seems more urgent, more demanding, and less forgiving. We must do it on the fly.

There are at least three things to take away from our discussion of communication as a process. The first thing is what is meant by defining communication as a process—namely, that communication is dynamic and that the parts interact and are interdependent. Second, when seeking to learn about communication, we tend to break it down into its parts. For example, when we get to persuasion in Chapters 7 through 12, we will talk about the source, distinct types of messages, and the audience. The implication of the idea of process is that it is critical that we do not lose sight of the fact that source, message, and audience are not separate but instead are interdependent. All communication is a joint function of the combination of these considerations embedded in a particular time sequence and situation.[9] Not only do all these considerations matter, but they also combine in unique ways in each act of communication. Finally, it is easy to lose sight of the over-time aspect of communication. Sequencing is important. For example, you might understand this chapter differently depending on if you previously read Chapter 1. What I say in this chapter might shape how you read the next chapter. In communication, order matters. The communication flow at one-time intervals has implications for later communication, and any given still frame or part of a sequence does not capture the entire sequential frames in motion, in context, and considering what came before.

SMCR: Source, Message, Channel, Receiver

According to Berlo, all communication involves a source, message, channel, and receiver. These are the four basic elements of the communication process, and they comprise his SMCR model of communication.

The *source* is the person or people who originate the communication. They have some idea to convey, meaning to share, and goal or goals to accomplish with others. To do this, they *encode* a *message*. Messages have physical properties like sounds, ink on a page, and pixels on the screen that can be heard, seen, and or/felt. Encoding is the process of source converting their thoughts into a message. The message is then sent over a channel. Berlo thought of our five senses (seeing, hearing, touch, smell, taste) as channels. You can also think of channels as different media: talking face-to-face, being live remote in video chat, reading a book, watching TV, texting, emailing, posting videos, etc. The *receiver* is the person being communicated to. The receiver is

---

9. In the previous chapter, I mentioned that I was not a fan of the ELM theory of persuasion. One reason is that it facilitates thinking about aspects of source credibility and argument quality as independent things. As we will see in Chapters 7, 8, and 9, they are not. For example, making strong arguments improves your credibility. Having credibility enhances the persuasive impact of evidence.

the audience. They *decode* the message, and communication has taken place. Decoding involves converting the message into thoughts in the receiver.

In the SMCR model, each of the four basic elements can be broken down further. Both sources and receivers have certain communication skills, attitudes, prior knowledge, and their own social systems and cultures. All of these will shape what they might want to communicate to whom, as well as how they might encode and decode messages. And surely, these are not the only things that matter. In later chapters, we will discuss other aspects of senders and receivers, such as sex, gender, and personality. The message contains content but also style, organization, grammar, and, if verbal, language. Finally, as mentioned previously, the channel involves both the human senses and the particular media. Media have different *affordances*. Radio is audio only, reading is visual, and television is audiovisual. Media can also be *synchronous* and *asynchronous*. For example, a telephone call is *synchronous,* while text messages can be more *asynchronous*. Some media are one-way, while other media allow a back-and-forth. Different media or modes of communication provide different access to nonverbal communication.

Complications

There is a potential logical consistency problem in reconciling our understanding of communication as a process and modeling it by breaking it down into its parts. We need to keep in mind that the parts all interact and that communication flows and is dynamic. Breaking things down into parts and parts of parts seems inconsistent with the very idea of communication as a process.

The most obvious concern with SMCR, however, is that it implies that communication flows one way from a source to a receiver. Some communication is indeed one-way. Examples are reading a book, watching TV, or reading a billboard or a road sign while driving. Other communication involves a back-and-forth with orderly turns. Email and text messaging often work this way. Communicators take turns alternating between the roles of sender and receiver. Communication that flows back the other way is often called *feedback*. As Gerald Miller observed, still other examples of communication involve simultaneous exchange.[10] People are at once both sending and receiving. For example, when you are talking to someone face-to-face, you can monitor their (mostly nonverbal) reactions while you are speaking.

SMCR lacks specifics on how exactly we encode and decode. These days, encoding is often called *message production or speech production*, and decoding is *message processing*. As we will see in the next chapter, how we do these things is not as straightforward as SMCR might imply. For example, people sometimes do not say what they mean but are still understood. Other times, people say something very straightforward but are misunderstood. And what does it mean to understand someone anyway?

Intrapersonal Communication?

Sometimes, the phase of intrapersonal communication is used in reference to communication with one's own self. An implication of the discussion so far is that I do not find this idea or terminology especially useful. A premise of this book is that communication is a between-people thing. It takes at least two people to communicate. We

---

10. Miller and Steinberg (1975).

can call what goes on in one person's own head thinking or cognition. If they are verbalizing their thoughts, this is thinking out loud.

Not *Not* Communicating

A final thing to discuss is the idea usually credited to the clinical psychologist Paul Watzlawick that one cannot not communicate. It is the case that sometimes, not saying something sends a message. However, not all behavior is communication. Communication is limited to actions that simulate meaning in the minds of others. Twiddling your thumbs when you are all alone does not communicate anything if no one else knows what you are doing. We can "not communicate," and we do things other than communicate much of the time, especially when we are sleeping.

Chapter Summary

- Communication was defined as a process in which people stimulate meaning in the minds of others through verbal and nonverbal messages.
- Defining communication as a process means that it is dynamic, flowing over time, and that its components are interdependent, creating something that cannot be understood from the parts in isolation.
- Berlo's SMCR model stands for source, message, channel, and receiver.
- SMCR is an oversimplification but nevertheless a useful starting point in understanding human communication.

The thing is, most of these ideas were around long before I ever learned them. This chapter covered the "oldie but goodie" building blocks starting point stuff of human communication. We have come a long way since Berlo, Watzlawick, McCroskey, and Miller authored the source materials for this chapter.

Next up, we peek at state-of-the-art thinking about what communication is and how we do it.

CHAPTER 3

Meme State Activation

[Dr. Levine's Voice]

My first real professor job was at the University of Hawaii. I loved living and teaching in Hawaii. I loved the beach. I loved the weather. I loved the mountains. I loved the food. I loved the island culture, and I loved the students. Most of all, I loved working with a great bunch of people. We were ohana. Ohana means family in Hawaiian. The only things I didn't like were the high cost of living and my low salary. I count leaving Hawaii to return to Michigan State as one of my biggest regrets in life, even though the move opened many other opportunities.

At the University of Hawaii, I had the great pleasure of meeting and working with my good friend Kelly Aune. This chapter is devoted to Kelly's ideas, or at least a very simplified version of them. For as long as I have known Kelly, he has argued that communication theory and research had the wrong priorities. He used the term "message processing" to describe his view, and he was frustrated that more communication research was not directed at what he saw as the main question facing the field of communication: How is it that we humans communicate? Over the 30 years that we have been friends, we continued this topic of conversion, and, over time, Kelly's ideas have evolved and taken shape. Last year, as Kelly was announcing his retirement, he and another professor from Hawaii (Jessica Gasiorek) published a book titled *Creating Understanding: How Communicating Aligns Minds.*[1] I'm proud to say that I was one of the first people to read an advanced copy. If you find the book in an online bookseller and look at the promotional materials, you will read:

> Gasiorek and Aune brilliantly tackle the Communication discipline's most central yet (ironically) most misunderstood problem: how is it that we do this thing we call communication? Creating Understanding has totally changed my understanding of understanding. This insightful work is a must read for those interested in the social science of communication.[2]

As their title implies, Gasiorek and Aune's thesis is that, more than anything else, human communication is about achieving some degree of understanding between communicators. They argue that how humans create **understanding** with other humans is the most fundamental issue for the academic study of communication. Understanding how we achieve understanding with others requires that we move beyond "code models" (involving encoding and decoding of messages) of communication like SMCR (covered in the previous chapter). It is not that code models are "wrong," but they are too simplistic and limiting, and they do not really capture the full breadth of what is really going on when we communicate. Current communication scholars like Gasiorek

---

1. Gasiorek and Aune (2021).

2. Levine (2020).

and Aune have access to modern work in neuroscience and linguistics that did not exist when Berlo was creating SMCR. In their view, messages are not the defining feature of communication, achieving understanding between people is. They do not even use the word message, and instead talk about **social stimuli**.

The Limitations of Code Models

Code models like SMCR work well enough for very literal verbal communication like Dr. Shebib and me authoring this book and you reading it. I am using the English language (a code) to translate (encode) my thoughts into words that you can read (decode). The source is me; the message is the words on the page; the channel is the book that you see (visual); the receiver is you, the reader. If all communication were like this book, SMCR would be good enough, although it would still lack detail on the neurophysiology of encoding and decoding. For example, as I type this sentence, I am "encoding," but just providing a label does not explain how I am doing it. The word decoding similarly lacks detail on the cognitive processes involved in reading, understanding, and remembering.

Code models get fuzzier when we think about less formalized, more everyday examples of communication. The thing is, people often do not say what they mean, but they are nevertheless understood. People imply things that are not said. People can communicate things they do not say at all. People can even mean exactly the opposite of what they say. Sarcasm is one example. Kelly's example is if he says to me, "Let's get a beer," I understand him to mean, "Let the two of us go together and get a beer for each of us." I know he is not suggesting that we share a beer, even though that is what he said.

Here is another example. Several years ago, I was on a search committee to hire a new professor. In a group discussion of the applicants, we were considering one candidate whose record of research looked quite strong on paper. Another member of the committee said matter-of-factly something like, "I have read their work. They have published lots of articles." On the surface, this indicates a favorable assessment. However, I heard it as implying that the professor making the comment had a low opinion of the applicant; specifically, they thought that the work was low quality. After the meeting, I followed up privately. As I guessed, the professor did have a poor opinion of the applicant and did think the applicant's work was low quality. But he said that he did not mean to encode that, and he was surprised that I noticed what he was thinking but not saying. Understanding this example from the perspective of a code model is a stretch at best. Code models do not explain how things are implied beyond the code or how people draw inferences about what might be implied.

The deficiencies of code models become even more apparent when we think about nonverbal communication. In my work on deception, I talk about the idea of demeanor.[3] **Demeanor** is the general way a person comes off. It is the overall impression. What I have discovered is that constellations of both verbal and nonverbal behaviors are given off in combination, and that is how they are perceived by others. Even something as basic as conveying that you are happy is often not so simple as just smiling. There is eye behavior involved, as well as other parts of the face, body movements, tone of voice, etc. That all works together in harmony with what is said. Of course, we can convey I am happy in a simple coded way by just saying "I'm happy" with just a smile or with a smiley face emoji. But that is not the only way we do so.

According to Gasiorek and Aune, the process of communication involves people presenting stimuli that activate **meme states** in others. People "construct, test, and refine mental models of joint experience,"[4] and when

---

3. Levine (2020), Levine et al. (2011).
4. Gasiorek and Aune (2021, p. 11).

peoples' mental models align, understanding is achieved. There is much to unpack here. Before we get there, we should note that the stimuli presented need not be a "code" or a "message," and the meme states that are activated need not be understood as "decoding." They can be, but they do not need to be.

Understanding as Converging Memes States

Gasiorek and Aune define **stimuli** as anything that can be sensed (something we can see, hear, smell, touch, or taste) and that evokes a response. **Social stimuli** are a subset of stimuli that come from and evoke responses in people. **Memes** "are people's mental renderings of concepts, ideas, and experiences."[5] Memes exist in people's heads while stimuli are observable. A meme is **activated** when it comes to conscious awareness; that is, it is brought to mind. Keep in mind that Gasiorek and Aune are using the term meme, like the biologist and author Richard Dawkins,[6] more so than its current use in popular social media.

Memes are not solitary. They exist in networks of memes in a person's mind. They are interconnected. Activating one meme can activate associated memes. There is what is called **spreading activation,** where one meme activates others, which activates others. A **meme state** is the memes that are currently activated in a context and time frame.

People have a type of meme state that can be called **situational models**. These are complex mental representations of how social episodes play out. You might have situational models for tailgating at football games, going out to the bar, attending class, or texting with friends or a specific friend.

We do not have direct access to other people's memes. Meme states and situational models exist only in each person's head and are unique to them. If we want to share them, we need to use social stimuli to do so. Seen this way, communication is about using social stimuli to activate memes and situational models in the minds of others.

Gasiorek and Aune define **understanding** as "two (or more) people experiencing entrainment of situational models as a result of at least one person's use of social stimuli."[7] The situational models and meme states in different people need not be identical. Understanding is not perfect. If you are getting the gist of this, then there is some understanding. It just needs to be good enough for the situation, acknowledging that some situations require more precision than others. Teaching you how to do brain surgery requires more understanding than explaining how to get to the nearest grocery store. Your doctor does not need to know exactly how you feel, just enough to diagnose and treat you. I just need to understand Gasiorek and Aune's book well enough to explain it to you. Fortunately, I can ask Kelly if I am getting it mostly right.[8] If you want a deeper understanding, you can read their book.

At this point, I want to digress a bit and discuss Alan Sillars's work on understanding.[9,10] Sillars points out that it is easy to confuse agreeing with another person and understanding them. Two people could have similar

---

5. Gasiorek and Aune (2021, p. 46).

6. Dawkins (2016).

7. Gasiorek and Aune (2021, pp. 51–52).

8. I actually did. Thanks, Kelly, for the feedback on this chapter!

9. Sillars found that married couples overestimated how much they agreed with their spouse and that perceived agreement rather than actual understanding or agreement contributed to marital satisfaction.

10. Sillars et al. (1984).

meme states just by chance. For example, you and your friend might have similar opinions about a particular artist. Sillar's point is that having a similar opinion is different than understanding the other person's opinion. You need to have a meme state about their meme state. We will get into this idea more in Chapter 20 when we talk about the theory of mind. Theory of mind plays an essential role in Gasiorek and Aune's account of how we communicate.

Communication works not only because there is a link between people's meme states and the social stimuli they enact but people understand that the stimuli they enact can impact other's meme states and that there is also a link between other people's meme states and the stimuli they give off. That is, I can think about what you are thinking and vice versa; there is a link between what I think and what I do, what I do can influence what you think (and vice versa), and I understand that what you think is linked with what you do. We understand that others want to communicate with us and that there is some content that they want to communicate. People then cooperate in making this happen. Gasiorek and Aune view communication as a fundamentally cooperative endeavor.

When people engage in communication, they **jointly pay attention to each other's social stimuli and treat each other's actions as relevant to their shared goal of seeking understanding**. Through past learning and experience, people associate stimuli with memes in memory. As they interact, people monitor the stimuli and "course correct" as needed. As Gasiorek and Aune put it, people "construct, test, and refine mental models of joint experience" as they go through the communication process.[11]

Goals and intentions are central to the communication process. Communication is a goal-directed activity. While seeking understanding is desired, we do more with communication than just achieving understanding. We get to know people, we establish relationships with others, we share knowledge and information, we seek to influence or persuade others, we seek to make good impressions on others, and we seek to comfort and support others, to name some common communication goals. And we can seek to accomplish more than one goal at the same time. Much of the rest of this book is about the goals we seek to accomplish with communication.

Our goals guide the social stimuli we give off. Also, our perceptions of other's goals and intentions shape how we respond to social stimuli of others. Goals, situational models, social stimuli, and meme state activation all function in combination.

Finally, context plays a critical role, according to Gasiorek and Aune. Social stimuli activate meme states in context, and which memes are activated depends on the larger **social context**. If I walked up to a stranger on the street and recited the last paragraph, they would wonder what I was talking about. If my wife says, "The dog is looking at me," this could mean quite different things depending on the context. If it is clear she is talking about our dog and we are talking face-to-face, then she wants me to take the dog out. If we are on Zoom, it might be that she needs to end the call and take the dog out herself. Or if it is someone else's dog, she feels threatened by a dog.

This is a huge simplification of Gasiorek and Aune's ideas. Furthermore, they provide just one of many modern approaches to understanding how it is that we humans communicate with each other. Another example focusing more on the production side is Steve McCornack's information manipulation theory 2.[12] My goal here was to provide you with a glimpse of how our understanding of communication as a process has evolved in the academic field of human communication. It is my hope that I sufficiently stimulated your curiosity and motivated a desire in you to learn more.

11. Gasiorek and Aune (2021, p. 11).
12. McCornack et al. (2014).

Chapter Summary

- Our collective understanding of how people communicate has progressed in recent years, especially with advances in neuroscience.
- Code models of communication like SMCR are overly simplistic.
- Achieving understanding with others is at the core of communication.
- We stimulate meaning (or meme states) in the minds of others, and understanding happens when meanings (or meme states) converge as the result of social stimuli in context.
- We do this through a context-dependent, goal-directed interactive process of anticipation, assessment, and refinement.

Next up, our attention turns to what I refer to as the three types of questions. I learned about the three types of questions from my professor, G. R. Miller, and understanding them is extremely helpful in understanding human communication.

CHAPTER 4

Three Types of Questions

[Dr. Levine's Voice]

Between the time I finished my master's degree at WVU and moved to Hawaii to be a professor, I'd earned my PhD at MSU. MSU was my first choice for furthering my studies because there were two professors at MSU who I wanted to learn from: Frank Boster and Gerald R. Miller. I had read Boster's research on compliance-gaining (Chapter 11), and I thought it was fantastic. Frank became my advisor and directed my doctoral dissertation. Miller was Boster's PhD advisor, so he became my academic grandfather. Like McCroskey, Miller was a larger-than-life presence in communication. I was very fortunate to have taken a couple of classes from him.

The field of human communication has changed quite a bit since Miller. Nevertheless, he originated many ideas that have stuck with me over the years. Most importantly, Miller taught me how to think about things in a more disciplined way. Good critical thinking skills never go out of style. One of the things I picked up from him is the topic of this chapter: three types of questions. My appreciation for these insights has grown over the years. I will pass them along to you and explain why they are useful.

According to Miller, there are three broad categories of questions that we might ask about communication.[1] The three types are questions of definition, questions of fact, and questions of value. All three are important. Understanding human communication necessitates engaging all three. However, each of the three needs to be approached differently. As we seek to enhance our understanding of human communication, the clarity of our thinking will benefit from knowing which type of question we are dealing with and being mindful of the challenges that each type of question entails.

Definitions

Questions of definition are an essential starting point in learning about any topic. Definitions, however, are especially relevant in learning about communication. Not only do we need useful definitions for various aspects of human communication, but the very act of defining a term is part of the communication process.

At issue is the meaning of words. Questions of definition ask things like: What does a particular word mean in a certain context? Is a given definition a good way to define this word or phrase? Which of several possible definitions serves us best for the purpose at hand?

We have already encountered many issues of definition in this book. A tentative working definition of communication by McCroskey was offered. Much of Chapter 2 was about defining communication as a process. In Chapter 3, social stimuli and meme states were defined. Of course, these are only a few examples.

---

1. This chapter is based on ideas originally published in Miller and Nicholson (1976).

For verbal forms of communication, having a shared definition is essential for communication. If you do not know what my words mean, I cannot (verbally) communicate with you very well. I lived in Korea for two years. Not speaking Korean limited my communication. Do not get me wrong. I could still communicate. I could do things like order food at a restaurant by pointing. But having a real conversation with anyone who did not speak English was impossible.

From the code model perspective, if words are the code that senders use to encode their thoughts and that receivers decode, then definitions are our cipher or codebook. If we are thinking in terms of social stimuli and meme state activation, definitions are essential for fine-tuning our own meme states and aligning our meme states with other meme states.

We need to take definitions very seriously and approach them in a thoughtful and disciplined way. Before studying under Miller, I often took definitions for granted and often did not give them much thought. They were things to memorize to pass a test or to look up in a dictionary when I was reading if I encountered a word I did not know. Definitions were a way to improve my vocabulary. After Miller, I never saw definitions the same way. I was more critical and less accepting of the definitions I encountered. I tried to be much more careful with my own definitions. This has helped me in teaching, writing, and, more generally, in life.

The first thing that Miller emphasized about definitions is that they are not true or false, and we must not approach them as if they were like facts. Words mean just what we mean by them, and this makes them arbitrary. Somebody just starts using a word a particular way, and sometimes it catches on. Dictionaries provide definitions that reflect common usages. People make up new words all the time. People also change how words are used, so definitions shift over time.

Many disagreements come down to people merely using words differently. People often think that how they are using the word is the correct way and other people are wrong. As an example, in my deception research, I use the term "truth-bias" differently than does Professor Judee Burgoon.[2] Neither of us has a special definition-conferring superpower that gives us exclusive rights to the word and its meaning. If we do not recognize that we are simply using different definitions, it makes it easy to talk past each other and miss the other's point. It also makes things difficult for our readers, who may come away confused if they read both of us and do not notice how we are using the same word differently.

Miller pointed out that much confusion is caused when different people use the same word to mean different things or different words to mean the same thing. The way out of these traps is to be clear about our definitions and apply critical thinking to identify potential points of confusion attributable to how words are being used. The negative consequences of this type of disagreement go away once we realize it for what it is. Disagreements and confusions stemming from different definitions are easy to fall into but also easy to avoid with a bit of awareness.

Although definitions are by their nature neither true nor false, Miller points out that **some definitions are more useful than others.** To understand what makes a definition useful, we need to be aware of the functions that definitions serve.

Definitions serve two main functions. The first function is communicative. Good, precise definitions allow people to understand what other people mean by a word. The other function has to do with what I call "clean

---

2. Dr. Judee Burgoon is among the most famous communication professors. I use her first name because her ex-husband Dr. Michael Burgoon was also a well-known communication professor. J. Burgoon is well-known for her work on expectations violation, nonverbal communication, and deception, especially interpersonal deception theory.

thought." Definitions are not just important for communicating with others; they also help us think about things. If you want to understand something, you need to know what it is and what it is not. Thinking about definitions forces us to consider the essence of something and its limits or boundaries.

There are two essential criteria to consider to accomplish these functions. The first criterion is **clarity**. Good definitions must be clear. Once wc define a term, we need to know what it means. If you read a definition and come away baffled, the definition is not doing its job very well. Good definitions clear the fog, not cloud the issue.

The second criterion is the **precision** of the definition in properly including and excluding examples. A good definition needs to include everything that is an example of the term being defined and exclude everything else. It needs to not be too broad or too narrow, and it needs to classify examples correctly.

For example, consider the term "vegetable." How do you define vegetables? If you say a vegetable is an edible plant, that is too broad. It would include fruits like strawberries. If you defined it as a green, leafy edible plant, that is too narrow. We need a definition of vegetable that includes all examples of vegetables and excludes all examples of nonvegetables. Of course, creating definitions that are just right while still being clear is often quite difficult. Nevertheless, the better we do on these two criteria, the more useful our definitions are.

Before moving on, categorizing things can also be thought of within the realm of definitions. This chapter is about the three types of questions. The next chapter is about the five perspectives. When I was in graduate school, professors debated how many types of compliance-gaining strategies or types of deception there are. Reasonable people can divide things into subtypes differently. When different sets of categories exist, one is not right or wrong. They are just different ways of sorting things.

Like with definitions, some category systems are better than others. They need to allow for proper and clear sorting of instances. Instances need to fit into just one category. There needs to be clear rules to know which category an instance falls within. All things in the same category need to have something in common that differentiates them from things in other categories. Finally, all instances need to fall into one category or another. When these conditions are met, a category system is **mutually exclusive and exhaustive**. Each category also needs a clear and properly inclusive and exclusive definition.

As a Matter of Fact

Unlike definitions and categories, **questions of fact** are true or false or have some quantifiable probability of being true. For example, I might want to know if it will rain tomorrow. If the local news says that there is only a 5% chance of rain, that is an issue of fact. Whether or not it rains at my house is also a question of fact. It will either rain or it will not. Time will tell. If we ask, what does a 5% chance of rain mean, that is a question of definition. Will it rain in only 5% of the area, or does it mean that on days with conditions like tomorrow, it will rain on only 1 in 20 such days? See the difference between questions of fact and definition?

One type of question of fact is an **empirical question**. These are questions that we can answer through observation. Systemic observations based on established social scientific methods like observational studies, content analyses, surveys, and experiments are particularly useful and relevant for this book. Each of these methods is an approach to answering empirical questions.

When we are dealing with research findings, these are issues of empirical fact. We saw several examples of empirically based factual statements in Chapter 1. Were there once other types of humans on earth? To what extent is social isolation related to mortality? How does social isolation stack up against other risk factors?

Keep in mind that facts can be wrong. We can think that things are true that are not. Not all research findings hold up. Although this might be counterintuitive, we are still dealing with questions of fact because, in principle, they are matters that are true or false, likely or unlikely. The quality of factual conclusions rests on the quality of evidence. Some evidence provides more certainty than other evidence. More on this in a bit.

When people disagree about matters of empirical fact, such disagreements can be resolved with **fact-checking** or research. Of course, people may not agree on which evidence is most relevant or on how to interpret the relevant data. It is also often the case that the evidence to date is not decisive in one way or another. Nevertheless, if it is a factual matter, it is, in principle, true, false, or probable-improbable.

Most of the factual knowledge about communication is probabilistic and normative in nature. Miller called this type of fact an **empirical generalization**. Empirical generalizations are statements based on observational evidence that hold "on average" or "typically" rather than invariably or universally. An example is the statement that men are taller than women. The difference between the average male (5 feet, 9 inches) and the average female (5 feet, 4 inches) is quite large statistically.[3] Nevertheless, some women are taller than some men.

This example of height differences based on binary biological sex differences highlights three important things to remember about empirical generalizations. First, the observation that some women are taller than some men does not mean that the more general conclusion that men are taller than women is wrong. Specific counterexamples do not disprove general trends. I call this error in reasoning an **instance disconfirmation**.

Second, we want to be careful about averages. Most people are not average. While it is the case that particulars do not disprove a probabilistic general claim, it is also the case that probabilistic general claims do not hold for all data points. Applying a true general statement too broadly is a fallacy called a **sweeping generalization** (more on this and other fallacies in Chapter 6).

Third, empirical generalizations usually have limits or boundary conditions. Findings may only apply under some conditions, hold for some categories of people, or emerge in some situations. When this is the case, the limiting factor is called a **moderator**. For example, using scary messages to persuade people to make less risky decisions works better on older people.[4,5] We say age moderates the effects of fear on persuasion.

One type of empirical evidence I use when available is **meta-analysis**. Meta-analysis was mentioned in the first chapter. Not all meta-analyses, however, are equally compelling. Nevertheless, when they are based on large numbers of individual studies from lots of different researchers and labs, and when the findings from the studies converge in a sensible manner, I consider conclusions based on meta-analyses to be a well-established fact. Meta-analyses are also a way to uncover moderators.

I consider evidence that is "significant" or "$p < .05$" highly fallible. If you read much research, you will encounter these terms. This type of statistical evidence is often misleading for reasons that go beyond the scope of this book.[6] For our purpose, isolated findings provide empirical evidence, but the evidence is weak until more findings converge. In communication research, many factual matters are not settled yet. Some findings suggest one thing; others suggest something else. As the book progresses, we will not only cover lots of research findings, but I will also try to contextualize the findings in terms of how well they are established.

---

3. I got the numbers from a Google search on January 1, 2021, and the numbers apply in the United States. How much confidence should we have in those numbers?

4. Frank Boster was my PhD advisor and G. R. Miller was Boster's advisor. That makes me a grandstudent of Miller's in academic linage.

5. Boster and Mongeau (1984).

6. See Levine et al. (2008) for discussion.

Values Are Important Too

Miller's third type is questions of value. Questions of value exist in the realm of ethics and morality. Questions of value encompass values, ethics, and morality, and for our purposes, these words are used interchangeably. They involve questions of right-wrong, good-bad, and should-shouldn't. What is the right thing to do? What is important to us?

Here is an example. As of this writing, my third most cited research article is a study on friends with benefits.[7] As you may know, friends with benefits refers to friends having sex with friends. The study was my student Melissa Bisson's master's thesis, and we coauthored an article together based on her thesis. She had heard of this new type of relationship[8] that she thought was a terrible thing, and she wanted to do research showing how harmful it was to have sex with a friend. I told her I would direct her thesis, but that research addresses questions of fact, not questions of value. We could ask research questions like what percentage of our students have had a friends-with-benefits relationship? Do friends-with-benefits couples stay friends, transition to romantic relationships, or lose their friends? These are factual questions, and in the research, we would stick to the facts. Our findings might inform value judgments, but that was a different type of issue.[9]

Our study provided a good example of the three types of questions. What is a friend-with-benefits relationship? This is a question of definition. How common are friends with benefits? This is a question of fact. The fact that our study went on to become a highly cited and influential article reflects a value judgment about what people find interesting, important, and citation-worthy.

Questions of value can be the most challenging of the three types. Good people can prioritize different values. We, of course, think that we are right, but so do others. Just because people have different ethical priorities does not make questions of value any less important. A premise running through this book is that a good communicator behaves ethically. But articulating what that means without being paternalistic, ethnocentric, or egocentric is tricky at best.

Here is an example of an ethical dilemma from my time as a professor in Korea. It was my perception that compared to the United States, elements of Korean culture are sexist. My opposition to sexism conflicted with my value of respecting other cultures. I was uncomfortable as a foreigner imperialistically criticizing the local culture. This dilemma required me to either prioritize one of my values over the other or risk hypocrisy.

There is a good deal of empirical research on how people approach moral decisions. Some of my favorite works are by the psychologist Jonathan Haidt and his moral foundations theory.[10] He has many good videos on YouTube, and I encourage you to watch a few of them.

According to Haidt, there are five core human values. Care-harm involves treating other people with kindness and compassion and not harming others. Fairness means treating people fairly (see Chapter 19). We should respect authority. There is in-group loyalty. The fifth is purity-sanctity. Haidt, who likes analogies and metaphors, thinks of these like our sense of taste. People have taste buds that detect sweet, sour, salty, bitter,

---

7. Bisson and Levine (2009).

8. Or maybe it was an old type of relationship with a new catchy label that came to public attention.

9. In case you are wondering what we found, a majority of the participants in our study, all college students, reported having had at least one friend with benefits. The relationships were casual and seldom developed into a romantic relationship. In fact, the point seemed to be having sex without a romantic commitment. People worried that their friend might develop romantic feelings, but mostly if that happened, it was not communicated.

10. Haidt (2013).

and savory. While everyone has these, people will differ in their taste for sweets, for example. One person might have a sweet tooth; another might like sour things. According to Haidt, we all have these five flavors of values, but different cultures have different cuisines to satisfy these, and there is also individual variation with cultures. If we wanted to expand the list, honesty might be a good addition. What do you think? Is honesty a core value distinct from the other five?

Haidt's research finds systematic differences between people who are liberal and conservative in the five core values. While everyone values all of them, liberals prioritize the first two: care-harm and fairness. Conservatives, in contrast, prioritize respect for authority, in-group loyalty, and purity-sanctity more so than liberals. This pattern holds up in liberals and conservatives all over the world. This might explain different reactions to police shootings, for example. Liberals are likely to key in on unjust harm, while conservatives might be more likely to see the injustice through the additional lens of respect for authority.

Haidt's five core values have important implications for approaching questions of value in communication. First, we need to understand that good people can prioritize values differently. When we communicate ethically, we need to consider our own ethical priorities and act accordingly. Further, when communicating, we need to think about our audience or the people who we are communicating with. Presuming other's priorities align with our own can lead to misunderstanding and can hamper achieving our communication goals.

Chapter Summary

- We need to understand the differences between questions of definition, fact, and value.
- Questions of definition deal with the meaning of words.
- Useful definitions are clear and precise.
- Questions of fact are, in principle, true or false, or more or less likely.
- Questions of value are about right and wrong, good and bad.

Next up, we will articulate five perspectives on human communication. The idea is that there is not just one way to look at human communication. We will look at communication from the biological, rewards and exchange, sociological, social-cognitive, and individual differences perspectives. Most of the chapters in the book involve one or more of these, so each is introduced next.

Five Perspectives on Human Communication

[Dr. Levine's Voice]

My parents never really understood what I did for a living. They knew I was a communication professor, that I taught college classes on topics like interpersonal communication and persuasion, and that I published research in academic journals. But, beyond that, they really couldn't explain it to their friends. At one point, in a story I still find amusing, my mother learned that I might have made a name for myself as a communication professor. My mother was having lunch with two cousins she had not met before. One of the cousins was a PhD student at the University of Pennsylvania. The cousin asked my mom if she was any relation to Timothy Levine, the communication professor. In my mom's telling, the cousin seemed quite impressed to be meeting my mother, implying that I was a famous professor. My mother was quite puzzled as to how this could be.

Part of my parents' lack of understanding might have been because communication classes and departments of communication did not exist in anything like their present form back when my parents were in college. My parents simply did not have the opportunity to take a class like Introduction to Human Communication. Communication is a young academic discipline. Even the oldest communication departments have only been around for about 70 years, give or take.

Even today, most students only learn about communication classes after they enroll in one. Many students come to college not knowing that being a communication major is even an option, much less what that might entail. As a chair of a communication department, part of my job has been explaining to others in the university what we offer. My experience is that it is not common knowledge.

Another reason for confusion is that communication departments vary quite a bit from university to university. Some are housed in colleges of arts and humanities, some are social sciences, and some have a professional school vibe and focus. Some communication departments contain all three. Communication classes may cover rhetoric, speech writing, performance studies, public relations, journalism, business communication, public speaking, radio, TV production, film studies, health communication, science communication, media effects, and/or social media, not to mention the various topics covered in this book. It is no wonder people get confused about the academic field of communication.

My own academic identity has at least two distinct faces. In one very important way, I am a communication professor who sees the world differently than, for example, a social psychologist. My disciplinary upbringing and affiliation led me to see human affect, cognition, and behavior from a communication-centered frame of reference. This first side of me understands communication as a topic of study distinct from other social and life sciences. On the other hand, I am a quantitatively oriented multidisciplinary social scientist. I try to read broadly outside my own field and specialties. You will see influences in this book from psychology, sociology, neuroscience, anthropology, philosophy, evolutionary biology, and other fields. Similarly, my research has appeal across many different academic fields and specialties. I am very much at peace with my academic duality, and I see no need at all to be exclusively one or the other. Still, I understand how this might be confusing. All this makes both me and my academic field hard to pigeonhole.

This chapter's thesis is that understanding human communication requires examining the topic from various perspectives. This is in part because communication is, at once, both a topic of its own and at the intersection of a variety of different academic fields. Here, I will focus on just five perspectives: biological, rewards exchange, sociological, social-cognitive, and individual differences. The idea is communication is inherently multidisciplinary and that no one academic approach or perspective is sufficient. In an important way, communication lies at the juncture of various life and social sciences. It fills the space between psychology and sociology, it has a biological and a cultural basis, and it is integral to all sorts of human activities, such as business, education, politics, religion, and entertainment.

Surely, these five perspectives are not the only way to split up the different approaches. Further, the approaches overlap. Moreover, they do not include all approaches to understanding human communication, such as rhetorical or critical perspectives. Nevertheless, the five described here are especially important to understanding the ideas discussed in this book. Here, each major perspective is given a shout-out, a brief explanation, and a few examples. The rest of the book will shift between these perspectives as we move from topic to topic.

The Biological Perspective

The biological perspective includes evolutionary explanations, genetics, neurophysiology, brain science, and hormones. We got our first bit of biological perspective back in Chapter 1 when talking about humans as a species. Humans evolved to communicate, and our ability to communicate has shaped our history. John Cacioppo's research on social isolation and mortality offered an evolutionary account arguing that feelings of loneliness serve the functions of motivating human contact and enhanced vigilance against threats. He also showed how social isolation lowered sleep quality, leading to biochemical changes that impair immune system function. My own truth-default theory is framed as an evolutionary imperative. Nothing is more important to humans, I argue, than efficient and effective communication. This requires believing in others. Otherwise, I argue, communication would bog down in uncertainty. Evolutionary arguments are also encountered in classes on interpersonal communication and personal relationships. The features of others that lead to romantic attraction and guide mate selection are argued to be explainable through an evolutionary approach to understanding human behavior.

Genetic accounts are often encountered in studying communication traits such as extroversion, aggressiveness, and communication anxiety. Twin studies show that identical twins are more similar in communication traits compared to fraternal twins. Half or even more of the variance in some communication traits might be heritable.[1] I caution, however, against presuming a hard and clear nature-nature divide in communication. First, the genes we are born with seem to impact our general tendencies (traits) more than any specific behavior. Further, to the extent that social behaviors have a heritable component, they do not seem to be attributed to any one or small sets of genes. Moreover, the environment and life experiences can govern how

1. Beatty et al. (2002).

genes are expressed. There is much interplay between our genetic presuppositions and our environment and lived experiences.

Some communication research also takes a neuroscientific approach. Michael Beatty and his coauthors, for example, looked at brain electrical activity using an electroencephalogram, comparing routine talk to giving someone directions.[2] Different patterns of brain activity were observed in the two message production tasks. In a second example, my friend Rene Weber's lab used functional magnetic resonance imaging brain scanning on people watching antidrug public service announcements.[3] Based on activity in two regions of the brain, they could tell if the messages were effective or not on a given person. Together, these studies show how communication research uses modern neuroscience to learn more about both the message production and message reception sides of the communication process.

Rewards and Exchange

Back when I was in college, the ideas of rewards and exchange formed a highly influential perspective on human communication. Over time, the social-cognitive perspective has displaced rewards and exchange in prominence. Although rewards and exchange are not the meta-theoretical powerhouses they once were, no understanding of human communication is complete without including this perspective as one among many.

The power of **rewards**, which might also be called positive reinforcement, is at the center of a set of principles from psychology called **operant conditioning**. Operant conditioning specifies that behavior that is reinforced tends to be repeated, and behavior that is punished becomes less frequent. Communication is obviously a behavior. It is something people do, a series of actions that we can observe. Rewards are desirable outcomes. Punishments are the opposite, undesirable, or aversive outcomes. Applied to communication, if you communicate in a particular way and that works well for you (i.e., the outcome or consequences are rewarding or favorable), then you are likely to do the same thing again next time. In contrast, if what you do does not work out well for you, you might be disinclined to do that the next time.

Operant conditioning, of course, plays a big part in how we learn things, including how we learn to communicate. We can learn that communicating in particular ways pays while other communication acts are bad ideas; the communication equivalent of learning not to touch the hot stove. As our learning about communication becomes more sophisticated, we learn that the action-reward connection depends on the situation. For example, it is especially important to be polite when meeting someone for the first time, or it is a bad idea to insult an especially vindictive person.

Operant conditioning also helps explain why we communicate. Communication is a way to get various tangible, social, or psychological goodies. Why does that person communicate the way they do? It was rewarding in their experience. Why doesn't a person do something? Maybe either they got punished for it in the past, or they just never got rewarded for it, so they did not learn to do that. Of course, rewards (and punishments) only take us so far in understanding communication behavior.

Sociologists took the ideas from operant conditioning and applied them to human interaction and relationships under the broad label of **social exchange theories**. The social exchange perspective starts out with basic operant conditioning; people seek rewards and avoid punishments or **costs**. In any exchange or interaction

2. Beatty et al. (2015).
3. Weber et al. (2014).

between people, there is an **outcome** based on rewards and costs. Outcomes equal the rewards minus the costs. If the rewards are greater than the costs, then the outcome is a profit, a net win. If the costs outweigh the rewards, it is a net loss. In line with the basic operant condition, people will repeat profitable interactions and seek to avoid costly ones.

The social exchange perspective extends these ideas in some important and insightful ways. For example, if two people interact with each other over time, the outcome of each interaction is less important than the profit over time—that is, the net gains (or losses) over many interactions. Consequently, people will suffer through unpleasant interactions so long as there is a bigger, more profitable outcome in sight. Thus, social exchanges are not one-offs but instead are ongoing with running tallies of gains and losses and future projections.

Second, **one fundamental principle of social exchange is that the payoffs must work out for all parties**. Everyone wants profit. However, in interactions where one person always wins, the people on the short end of the reward will find someone else to exchange with. Consequently, it is essential for making exchanges work that all participants are happy with the exchange. People in exchange relationships must balance their own profit and be a profitable person for others to exchange with.

So, what might be exchanged? Anything of value. I can exchange money for a cup of coffee or much more money for a new automobile. **We can also exchange intangible things like favors, knowledge, respect, or affection.**

A final basic principle of social exchange is that **whoever controls more of the things that are valued has more power in an exchange relationship.** If you control things other people want, they need you. You can set the terms of the exchange. Of course, people are free to "walk away" and exchange with someone else if there is a better deal to be had elsewhere or if they can simply live without what you have to offer.

The Sociological Perspective

Social exchange is not the only perspective from sociology useful in understanding human communication. Chapter twelve is devoted to the ideas of sociologist Irving Goffman. The chapters on fairness and networks also take a sociological perspective. We will cover those ideas in those chapters.

At its heart, the sociological perspective on human communication recognizes and emphasizes the truism that all communication exists within a larger **social ecosystem**. Communication takes place within cultural and subcultural systems (see Chapter 15) and within social intuitions like governmental systems, educational systems, economic systems, and religious institutions. When we talk to friends, there are overlapping friends of friends. Every family has its own family dynamics. The same is true at work, where there are formal chains of command and informal rumor mills. There are norms, politeness rules, and conventional ways of acting to follow or violate. While we learn about communication, we do not want to miss the forest by paying attention to just the individual trees. The sociological perspective reminds us to pay attention to the bigger social picture.

The Social-Cognitive Approach

If there was an academic popularity contest among the various perspectives, the social-cognitive view would be the odds-on favorite and has been at least since the 1990s. The core idea is that if you want to understand how people communicate, you need to know how people think. **Cognition** just means thinking. Social cognition is people thinking about people or people thinking in social situations. This is not the brain science we talked about from the biological perspective. Here we are talking about the mind, not the brain.

We got our first big peek into the social-cognitive way of looking at communication in Chapter 3 and meme state activation and achieving understanding. That chapter was about as socially cognitive as it gets.

There will be two more chapters that are pure social-cognitive perspective through and through. These are Chapter 18, about uncertainty and attributions, and Chapter 20, about the theory of mind and empathy. **Uncertainty** is what it sounds like. It involves not knowing what to expect or not knowing why things are happening. **Uncertainty reduction theory** is a communication theory that says we use communication to be less uncertain. Of course, there is much more to it. **Attributions** are about how people make sense of what others are doing, as Sally attributes Susan's complaining to her sour personality. **Theory of mind** is about understanding other people have minds and perspectives different from our own. Finally, **empathy** includes understanding other people's perspectives, catching other people's feelings, and caring about others. All of these are important for human communication. They also all involve thinking and the mind.

As I write this, it occurs to me that although this chapter is about five different perspectives, the chapter has a very cognitive flavor overall. The very idea of shifting between different perspectives—looking at our topic from this angle and that vantage point, and with a diverse set of assumptions and priorities—is a cognitive exercise and not an especially easy one at that. There is not just one way to see the world, and within our mind is the ability to shift between views. This is a cognitive skill that I encourage you to practice.

Individual Differences

The final perspective is that of individual differences. Earlier today, I was reading an online discussion entry about an assigned research article that one of my students wrote. In this student's opinion, as she expressed it, everyone is different, and it all depends on what is important to the person. Her view captured the essence of an individual difference perspective. *People are different, and if you want to understand communication, you need to know about the people involved.* You might want to know about their culture (Chapter 15), if they are male, female, or nonbinary (Chapter 16), or about their personality (Chapter 22).

Chapter Summary

- There are many different perspectives on understanding human communication, and achieving understanding requires looking at it in diverse ways.
- Five perspectives were briefly summarized: biological, rewards and exchange, sociological, social-cognitive, and individual differences.
- The biological approach sees humans as biological entities that evolved to have genes, have brains, and have hormones. All these play a role in communication.
- The rewards and exchange perspective grew out of operant conditioning in psychology. Behavior that is rewarded is repeated. This is how people learn and why people do things.
- The sociological perspective reminds us that human communication exists within a social ecology, and thus, we need to be mindful of the role of cultures, norms, and other social structures so that we do not lose sight of the big picture.
- The social-cognitive view seeks to understand how people think.

- The individual difference approach reminds us that people are all different, and one size does not fit all.

This concludes the opening set of chapters that together introduce basic ideas in human communication. The next set of chapters contains a series of topics relating to persuasion and social influence. The first of these, and next up, is a transition chapter on sound arguments.

Unit II

Communication and Influence

CHAPTER 6

Sound and Strong Argument

[*Dr. Levine's Voice*]

Back when I was a new professor just starting out at the University of Hawaii, I was looking to establish myself in the academic field of human communication. I was trying to do important, high-quality, influential research, and I wanted to publish my work in the top communication journals. Publishing in the most prestigious journals is seen by professors as evidence (Chapter 7) that one is doing top-notch research, and it adds to one's professional credibility (Chapter 8). More than that, top journals reach larger audiences than less prestigious outlets, and thus, they add visibility.

Early in my career, I was fortunate to place several articles in one of the top journals, *Communication Monographs (CM)*.[1] It took me longer to start publishing in the other top journal, *Human Communication Research (HCR)*. My first article in *HCR* was an experiment on listening and memory with a student named Todd Thomas, who was interested in listening.[2] Our basic idea was that most listening tests had people listen to something, and then they were tested on listening by asking them to recall what they had listened to. Our argument was that this procedure was testing both listening and memory. Listening and memory are two different things! Our experiment was designed to parse listening from memory. It was a cool experiment.

Much to my surprise and initial horror, Robert Bostrom, a big-name communication professor and leader in listening research, took exception to our article. Worse, he published a criticism of our work! Todd and I were invited to write a short rejoinder providing our response to Professor Bostrom's criticisms.[3] As it turns out, this was the first of many published back-and-forth academic arguments for me. I have been the critic, and, like with Bostrom, I have been on the receiving end defending my arguments. I have debated with Judee Burgoon on three occasions[4] and Aldert Vrij twice[5] regarding various issues in deception research, with Infante and his colleagues about argumentativeness and verbal aggressiveness,[6] and with Bill Gudykunst and Min Sun Kim about cross-cultural communication and identity.[7] Many of these arguments were published in top journals.

The relevance of this story, of course, is that this chapter is about arguments and argumentation. By the end of this chapter, I want you to know why **sound argument** is important and what makes an argument sound or **strong**. My story is relevant to the first of these goals, why the strong and sound argument is important. A strong and sound argument is about good critical thinking and effectively communicating good critical thinking.

---

1. Levine and McCroskey (1990) was my first article in *CM*. (Steve McCornack and I had two more that year and a third in 1992.)

2. Thomas and Levine (1994; I now have about 25 articles in *HCR* and 19 in *CM*).

3. Thomas and Levine (1996).

4. Levine and McCornack (1996), McCornack et al. (1996), and Park and Levine (2015).

5. Levine and Blair (2018) and Levine et al. (2018).

6. Levine et al. (2012).

7. Levine et al. (2003).

Understanding sound arguments let me see which of my critic's points were reasonable and good and which were flawed and how so. That is, understanding sound arguments equipped me to debate effectively. It is about critically assessing if incoming arguments are sound and creating sound arguments of your own. Both the sending and receiving sides of arguments are important.

Keep in mind that these were published debates. Lots of other people read them, and surely, people formed impressions of me based on what they read. In the debate with Bostrom, I could appear to be the young professor who got in over his head and was taken to task by the senior professor; I could be a new person who could hold his own; I could be an unusually smart and insightful young scholar with the bright future. How Todd and I responded had consequences for our careers.

In case you are wondering how the story ends, Bostrom's criticisms were not too hard to address. He made some good points, which we acknowledged, but those were ancillary to our main point. Most of his criticisms were based on misunderstanding our claims. If our work had been as he described, his criticism would have been sound. However, because the criticism was aimed at points we did not actually make, his argument was a **strawman** (or straw person, if you prefer). In other words, his points were **counterfactual**, based on something that might have happened but didn't. We just respectfully pointed it out for what it was and contrasted that with our actual original argument. We showed how his points demonstrated the need for and importance of our work.

Why Sound Arguments Are so Important

Critical thinking and sound arguments are quintessential abilities of the educated person. The educated person applies critical thinking (evaluates content arguments) to incoming information and communication. Sound argument is the outward expression of good critical thinking. Understanding sound arguments and being able to differentiate between assertions, flawed arguments, strong arguments, and sound arguments goes a long way toward being able to think critically and toward communicating in a way that reflects strong critical thinking skills.

Communicating with strong and sound arguments marks you as an educated person. Not everyone, however, recognizes strong and sound arguments when they see them. People confuse things like authority, likability, confidence, or sheer assertiveness with argument quality. For those people who know and recognize sound arguments when they hear them, however, being able to construct them marks you as being among those who can and do.

Strong and sound arguments are not about winning arguments. Chapters 7 through 13 are all about influencing people. Argument skills are part of the persuasion toolbox, but sound arguments will not persuade people who either lack the critical thinking skills to understand the argument or people who, for whatever reason, are set in their ways and are not going to change their minds regardless of the reasons. Sound argument is for the people who want to be factually accurate, logical, and ethical. It is a communication style that is genuine and leads to respect. Moreover, argument skills are not just about making arguments. Argument skills are also essential for evaluating the communication you encounter.

What Is an Argument?

An **argument** is a set of premises that support or entail a conclusion.[8] Arguments are made up of **propositions**. A proposition is what a declarative sentence expresses. They are claims of fact (see Chapter 4) and, in principle, can be judged as true or false.

Arguments contain two types of propositions. A **premise** is one of the reasons being advanced in support of the conclusion. The premises of an argument are the complete set of reasons being advanced for believing the conclusion. A **conclusion** is a statement of the point for which one is arguing. It is the **claim** being made. A claim without supporting reasons is an **assertion**.

What Makes an Argument Sound?

An argument being sound (or not) applies to deductive arguments. A valid **deductive argument** is one in which the conclusion follows necessarily from the premises. If one accepts the premises of a deductive argument as true, then one must accept the conclusion as true as well. A deductive argument is **sound** when it is both logically **valid** and **the premises are true**.

This sets up two criteria for evaluating an argument: (1) evaluating the factual basis of the premises and (2) assessing the logic connecting premises to the conclusion. A valid argument (meaning it is logically fine; the premises, if true, lead invariably to the conclusion) can be unsound if a premise is false. An argument is neither sound nor valid if the premises are true, but the conclusion does not follow from the premises (it is not logical). Of course, an argument is also unsound and invalid if a premise is false, and the conclusions do not follow from the premises.

Examples

Consider the following set of propositions.

1. All birds have beaks.
2. I saw an animal with a beak.
3. Thus, I saw a bird.

Is this even an argument?
Which statements are the premises, and which is the conclusion?
Is this argument sound, valid but unsound, or invalid and unsound?

Yes, this is an argument. There are premises (a and b) that appear to lead to the conclusion (c). It is, however, unsound. Presuming that premises (a) and (b) are true, the conclusion (c) does not necessarily follow. I might see an animal with a beak that is not a bird, like a turtle or octopus. Consequently, it is invalid and unsound.

Here is another.

---

8. I adapted this definition and the content in this section from Professor Franklin J. Boster's lecture notes from when he and I co-taught an argumentation class at MSU.

1. All birds are red.
2. I saw something red.
3. Thus, I saw a bird.

This time, the problems include both a false premise and the link between the premise and the conclusion. This is unsound because not all birds are red, and even if they were, not all red things are birds.

One more.

1. All birds have beaks.
2. I saw a bird.
3. Thus, the bird I saw had a beak.

How about now? A quick Google search leads me to believe that premise (a) is true. I know that I did indeed see a bird. Therefore, you can correctly presume that the bird I saw did indeed have a beak. This seems like a sound argument. However, what if the bird I saw had a beak, but it broke off prior to my sighting?

What Makes an Argument Strong?

An **inductive argument** is one in which the conclusion follows from the premises with some degree of probability, but the truth of the conclusion is not guaranteed by the truth of the premises. Usually, this involves going from instances to generalizations. A quite common example of this is applying findings from research. For example:

1. I have done more than two dozen deception detection experiments.
2. On average, the participants in each one of my deception detection experiments were truth-biased. That is, in every study so far, participants are more likely to believe someone was honest than to think they were lying.
3. Therefore, generally speaking, people are truth-biased.

What do you think? Do you accept the conclusion (c)? Should you? Inductive arguments such as the one above can be judged as being more or less strong, but they cannot be judged as being valid or invalid in the way of deductive arguments. The same rule regarding the accuracy of the premises applies. If the premises are false, we can reject the argument as unfounded. Game over. In this case, premises (a) and (b) are true. Conclusion (c) seems to be the case based on the available data, but we cannot be sure. Maybe future research will suggest otherwise. The conclusion is tentative. The more data behind it, the stronger the argument. The more exceptions there are, the weaker the conclusion. When 24 studies all find the same thing without exception, the conclusion is strong (but not certain).

Informal Fallacies

A **fallacy** is an argument that is unsound and misleading. The informal means that we are using language, not symbolic logic. This chapter has been about **informal arguments**. The two components that make an argument fallacious are that it is incorrect, flawed, or unsound and that it is not so obviously so. A fallacious argument is a flawed argument masquerading as a sound or a strong argument.

Informal Fallacies and be sorted into at least three categories. The first type is **fallacies of ambiguity**. This might involve words with multiple meanings that shift meanings as the argument progresses, words taken out of context, words where multiple meanings are possible, etc. We can separate ambiguity from vagueness, although both are relevant. **Ambiguity** is when a proposition has more than one meaning. **Vagueness** is when terms lack clear definitions. Both ambiguity and vagueness need to be avoided in constructing a sound or strong argument.

I used the example of research supporting the idea of truth-bias previously. The critical reader will ask, what is truth-bias? How is it defined? Do all the studies supporting it define it in the same way? If not, might the differences in definition make the claim of consistency of support fallacious?[9]

The second type is **fallacies of presumption**. These involve overlooking some facts, distorting the facts, or having hidden assumptions. Fallacies of presumption involve insufficient, false, or misleading premises. I see examples of this all the time when reading academic books and articles. A claim is made, and a list of references is provided in support. However, conflicting findings are not mentioned, making a claim less well supported than it appears.

Third, **fallacies of relevance** have to do with the logical link between the premises and the conclusion. These include personal attacks, appeals to authority, and appeals to common practice, among other things. The Bostrom criticism in the story that opened this chapter was an example. Many of his criticisms were not relevant to our claims.

Evaluating Arguments

The three types of fallacies, as well as the definitions of sound and strong argument, set up the three basic ways to evaluate an argument.

1. Are the premises and conclusions clear?
2. Are the facts and premises true, reasonable, or well supported?
3. Does the conclusion follow from the premises?

When you encounter an argument, either someone else's or your own, ask the three questions above. These will go a long way toward making you a better critical thinker and help you make more compelling arguments.

Three Additional Bits of Advice

When you are arguing, my first additional suggestion is to pick your battles. I really have two things in mind here. The first is if the issue is important and worth the effort. Sometimes it can be tempting to point out a fallacy

---

9. I define truth-bias as the tendency to believe another person independent from their actual honesty. In my experiments, I always score it the same way; number of times a person thinks another person is honest divided by the total number of judgments they make. While I am consistent in my use of the term, other researchers adopt different definitions. This can make arguments between us confusing unless the different definitions are recognized.

when you see one. Do not be a jerk or argumentation show-off. Not all weaknesses need to be pointed out. The second part of picking battles involves picking which conclusions to argue for. Some conclusions are easier to defend than others. There are good reasons supporting them. Pick conclusions that allow for defense by sound argument—that is, conclusions based on true and logical premises. Also, pick conclusions that are difficult for a critic to counterargue. The idea is that you get to choose when you argue and what you argue for. Stake out the argumentative high ground.

Second, take your time. Don't rush. Think things through. Double-check your evidence and your logic. Think about what you might be missing. Is there something you have not thought of that undercuts your position? When I am in academic debates, I like to imagine that the person I am arguing with is supersmart. I think, though, what the most challenging opponent might produce to counter my arguments. Then, I either set rhetorical traps (leave apparent openings I know I can defend) or preempt them by showing upfront that I considered the alternatives and had good reasons for not accepting them.

Finally, practice. Critical thinking and constructing sound arguments take practice. You need to exercise your cognitive abilities just like muscles and cardiovascular conditioning. Get used to questioning premises, recognizing ambiguities, and spotting logical gaps.

Chapter Summary

- An argument is a set of premises that support a conclusion.
- Arguments have two parts: premises and conclusions.
- Understanding arguments is essential for being an educated person.
- A sound argument is one in which the premises are true, and the conclusions follow from the premises.
- A fallacy is an argument that is unsound and misleading.

Next, we will talk about the related topic of evidence. The focus, however, is shifting. In this chapter, the focus was on making sound and strong arguments. The next several chapters focus on being persuasive. How do we change people's minds and get them to do things? One way of persuading people is by using evidence. We will look at types of evidence and when evidence is effective in achieving persuasion.

CHAPTER 7

Evidence

[Dr. Levine's Voice]

As I am writing this chapter, the COVID-19 pandemic in the United States seems to be on the decline.[1] Apparently, the main reason for the decline in cases and fatalities is that the vaccines have been effective. I can quite happily say that I am fully vaccinated and have been for a few months now. I feel fortunate that the university I work for was quite good at making vaccinations available to faculty. I got vaccinated as soon as I could. Vaccines were not mandated. Getting vaccinated was my choice. Did I make the right one? What influenced my decision?

My decision to get vaccinated was not purely a matter of evidence, but evidence played an outsized role.[2] There were at least three questions of fact that guided my decision. The first was the risk of not being vaccinated. If I did not get vaccinated, what were the chances of me getting infected, and if I did get infected, how likely were adverse outcomes like temporary discomfort of the symptoms, hospitalization, long-term ill effects, and even death? Second, if I did get vaccinated, how protective would it be? That is, how much would the vaccine lower my risks of COVID-19 and its ill effects? Third, what were the potential risks of the vaccine, including potential side effects, allergic reactions, etc.?

As an active researcher, I was able to understand the modeling and clinical trials.[3] For me, the decision seemed straightforward. COVID was not a disease I wanted. It probably would not kill me if I got it, but there was a chance that it could. There was a much better chance that it would be unpleasant. All the early evidence on the effectiveness of the vaccine pointed to remarkably good efficacy. It reduced the chances of getting COVID-19 by quite a bit, and for those vaccinated people who still got infected, the symptoms were reduced considerably. The side effects of the vaccine were minor compared to the symptoms of COVID-19. Based on my understanding of the evidence, I was persuaded to get vaccinated as soon as possible.

As I write this, there seems to be more vaccine available than there is demand. Almost two-thirds of the adults in my state have not yet been vaccinated; thus, there seem to be many people who made a different choice than I did. There have most certainly been efforts to get people in my area vaccinated. What determines if people are persuaded or not? What should public health professionals be doing to persuade people? The next several

---

1. This was true when I first wrote this sentence. By the time I finished writing the chapter, it looked like there might be a resurgence due to a new more transmissible variant and low vaccination rates in some regions. By the time you read this, maybe the world will know how things turned out (or maybe things will still be in flux).

2. Besides questions of fact (as informed by evidence), there were also questions of value. I felt I had an ethical obligation to my fellow humans to slow the spread if I could. For me, this meant masking in public and getting vaccinated as soon as it was my turn.

3. This is my understanding of the evidence at the time I am writing. I'm not a doctor, and this is not a professional medical opinion. Further, the evidence is not all in yet and things can change.

chapters look at communication tools in the persuasion toolbox and discuss which persuasion tools work well for which situations. First up is what got me to want to get vaccinated: evidence.

Before getting into the main parts of the chapter, my story here points to a couple of important things about evidence and persuasion to keep in mind as you read on. First, evidence can persuade people, as was the case for me. Second, strong evidence does not guarantee persuasion. Clearly, many people are deciding not to get vaccinated. People can understand the same evidence differently, ignore evidence, or doubt evidence. Finally, there are typically other persuasive forces at play, such as preexisting values and social pressures from others, that can counteract even the strongest evidence.

Rational Appeals

Evidence, together with a strong and sound argument discussed in the last chapter, form the basis of the **rational approach** to persuasion. When evidence and sound arguments are the force behind or *mechanism* of persuasion, we can call these strategies **rational appeals**.

The rational approach is the thinking person's strategy because it requires conscious critical thinking on both the persuader and the target of the persuasion. It is an ethical approach to persuasion, and to the extent that the arguments are sound or strong and the evidence is of high quality, it usually leads to good and reasonable decisions. Using rational appeals has the bonus of increasing the credibility (see next chapter) of the people who use them. Alternatives to rational appeals include emotional appeals (Chapter 9) and persuasive strategies based on mindless decision rules (Chapters 10 and 11).

Defining Evidence and Types of Evidence

Evidence, as applied to persuasion, refers to "*factual statements originating from a source other than the speaker, objects not created by the speaker, and opinions of persons other than the speaker, that are offered in support of the speakers claims.*"[4] It follows from this definition that while evidence can be either factual or opinion, it must come from a person or entity other than a source. Thus, if I am trying to persuade you, for example, that the effective use of evidence is an important communication skill, offering my own professional opinion would not count as evidence. However, if I quote McCroskey's opinion, that would be evidence.

As the preceding definition implies, evidence can be considered as falling into two types: factual and testimonial. **Factual evidence** involves a matter of fact—that is, things that are true or false, happened or not, or have some probability of occurring. Examples of factual evidence include research findings, statistical evidence, eyewitness accounts, and physical evidence in the courtroom, such as DNA, fingerprints, and bloodstain patterns.

Just because the evidence is factual does not mean that it is true or valid. Sometimes, the results of studies do not hold up. DNA results can be contaminated. Eyewitness accounts are notoriously unreliable and can result in false convictions. The category of factual evidence is an issue different from the quality of the evidence, and both are different from the persuasive effectiveness of evidence. Identifying evidence as factual simply means that it is making a factual point (see Chapter 4 about issues of fact).

---

4. McCroskey (1969, p. 2).

Testimonial evidence, on the other hand, involves opinions. Examples include product reviews, political endorsements, and expert testimony in the courtroom.

Not too long ago, I was retained by defense counsel in a federal conspiracy case. The case turned on whether the defendant was part of the conspiracy or a victim of it. The prosecution's case was that the defendant had to know, despite the lack of affirmative evidence, that he was an active participant. There were no emails of him plotting nor bank records of him profiting. There was no factual evidence of guilt. The prosecution's argument was basically that no one could be that gullible. He had to be in on it. I wrote a brief as a deception researcher, citing research (factual evidence) showing people's vulnerability to deception and offering my professional opinion (testimonial evidence) that it would not be at all surprising or unusual for someone in the defendant's position to be fooled and not realize that criminal behavior was going on. Fortunately for the defendant, the charges were dropped. I tell this story because the case shows examples of both types of evidence.

Quality of Evidence

Judging the quality of evidence is much like judging the quality of an argument (Chapter 6). The quality of the evidence is a matter of its **relevance** and its **validity**. The validity of evidence, in turn, depends on the **correspondence** with facts and its logical **coherence**. That is, evidence is of high quality when it is relevant to the point of the persuasion, it is consistent with known facts, and it is logically consistent (some aspects do not contradict other aspects).

When Evidence Works Best

Let us start with a couple of things that do not really matter. First, both factual evidence and testimonial evidence can be highly persuasive or can fail to persuade. **One type is not superior to the other in persuasive impact.** This said, some persuasive topics lend themselves better to some types of evidence than other topics. I prefer factual evidence regarding vaccines but testimonials in trying a new restaurant.

Instead, **the persuasive power of evidence rests on four main things: source, quality, quantity, and the audience.**

First, **evidence is more effective when it comes from a credible source** (see Chapter 8). Does the evidence come from a prestigious source like a famous professor or a leading academic journal? Is the source of the evidence impartial, unbiased, and trustworthy? For example, when evaluating vaccine effectiveness, I might trust research that was collected by the Centers for Disease Control and Prevention over research done by the drug company that made the vaccine and stands to profit from it. On a restaurant review, I want to know that the person ate there and was not paid for their review. In doing the research for this book, I rely much on researchers who I think do high-quality work and are thus credible in my opinion.

Second, **higher quality evidence (validity and relevance) is more persuasive than lower quality evidence.** However, this requires both that the evidence is understandable, and that the audience is paying attention to detail. If the evidence is not understandable or if the audience is not focusing on it, then quality does not matter because the audience cannot assess it.

Third, the sheer amount of evidence sometimes matters. **Presenting more evidence is better than less when either the quality is high, or the audience cannot judge the quality of the evidence.** If the quality of the evidence is high, then having more high-quality evidence is better than less. Alternatively, if the audience cannot judge the quality, the audience can usually still judge the quantity, and more is better.

Here is an example of the quantity and quantity of evidence. Imagine I am on a committee to hire a new professor. If it is my own field, I will look and see if they have been published in high prestige journals. I might even read their work. If the quality is good, then I will prefer the candidate who has more high-quality research to one with less. But, if I am on a committee hiring a new chemistry professor, I am not able to judge the quality of the work, so I will prefer the candidate with the most publications.

Fourth, the persuasive of evidence depends on two audience features: involvement and prior familiarity. **Audience involvement** refers to the extent to which the topic is important to the audience, how much the audience cares, and if the topic impacts the audience in important ways. Evidence and rational appeals work better with more involved audiences. Second, evidence works best when it has news value to the audience—that is, the audience was previously unfamiliar with the evidence.

Using Citations in Academic Work

Besides persuasion, evidence is important for students and academics in another way: using citations in papers. There is an art to using citations.

First up, there are two main reasons to use citations. The first is to acknowledge intellectual property and avoid plagiarism. This is giving credit where credit is due. If you are using someone else's words, you put them in quotes and cite where you found the quote. For example, when I used McCroskey's definition of evidence earlier in the chapter, I quoted and cited it. The same is true for ideas.

The second way citations are used is as evidence. If you are making a factual claim, the citation directs the reader to the source of the evidence. When using citations as evidence, the relevance and accuracy of the evidence are critical.

Chapter Summary

- Evidence and arguments are two types of rational appeals.
- Evidence can be factual or testimonial.
- The persuasiveness of evidence rests on the source of the evidence, the quality of the evidence, the amount or quantity of the evidence, audience involvement, and audience prior familiarity.

The next chapter examines source credibility. The source of a persuasive message matters, and more credible sources are more persuasive than less credible sources. As we will also see, source credibility and evidence often go together. Credible sources make the evidence more persuasive, and the effective use of evidence can boost source credibility.

CHAPTER 8

Source Credibility

[*Dr. Levine's Voice*]

In previous chapters, I mentioned going to graduate school at WVU. There, I took two classes from Professor Lawrence "Buddy" Wheeless. Wheeless did this thing I had not observed previously from other professors. It really impressed me. When a student asked a question, he would answer by not only explaining the gist of what research had found but by describing the findings in remarkable detail. On top of that, he provided the citation off the top of his head. He would say something like, "Well Knapp et al., I think that was 1973 in *Speech Monographs*, maybe issue three, found consistent patterns in how people say goodbye." I remember wondering how he could do that. It conveyed a mastery of the literature. Clearly, Wheeless was a professor who knew what he was talking about.

I asked him to be my advisor, and he directed my master's thesis. In graduate school, after students conduct the research that will be their master's thesis or doctoral dissertation, they do a "defense." The student and their advisor put together a group of professors called the student's committee, and during the defense, the committee questions the student. The student explains and defends their work (hopefully with sound argument and good evidence) and demonstrates that they have mastered the subject matter and deserve their degree.

In preparation for my thesis defense, Wheeless made sure I had an encyclopedic knowledge of the work I cited. As his student, I was expected to show the other professors that I knew what I was talking about. Wheeless made sure I could do with my thesis topic what he could on the topics that he taught—convey credibility.

After my defense, I went out drinking with Wheeless and McCroskey (who was on my committee). One of the other members of my committee was a new young professor at the time, and my thesis defense was her first committee as a professor. I expressed relief at passing. McCroskey said that he and Wheeless were not worried about how I would do. They were sure I would answer the questions well, and they thought my thesis was strong. They were more interested in how the new professor would do in questioning me. I was not the only one who needed to establish credibility. This story stuck with me, and it exemplifies both the importance of source credibility and some ways of building it.

Definition

Source credibility is the extent to which others find a communicator *believable*. It is *perceived believability*. My credibility is how much you find what I say and write believable. It is important to keep in mind that credibility is a *perception*. It is in the eyes of the beholder (or ears of the listener). I, or any communicator for that matter, can only be credible to the extent that you and others accept what I am communicating. Do you see me as an honest, reliable, and knowledgeable source of information? Part of my credibility is the impression that I am giving off. As we will see, there are things people can do to boost their credibility in the eyes of others. A key idea here is that credibility depends on how a source is viewed by others, and thus, source credibility resides in the audience or receiver.

Ethos, Pathos, Logos

You may have heard of the famous Greek philosopher Aristotle. He described three elements of effective persuasion: ethos, pathos, and logos. Ethos translates into the modern-day concept of source credibility, and thus, the idea that source credibility is an important consideration in persuasion is often credited to him. Much of the early research on credibility in the field of communication was done under the label of ethos by McCroskey, who had a background in rhetoric.

Pathos refers to using emotion in a person, which is covered in Chapter 9. Logos, in contrast, involves evidence (Chapter 7) and rational arguments (Chapter 6). Good persuasion can involve all three.

Early Research

The earliest social science research on source credibility was done by people like Carl Hovland.[1] He was a psychologist at Yale who worked with the U.S. Army during World War II on propaganda and persuasion. Early experiments went something like this. Research participants would read or hear persuasive messages. The messages were the same but attributed to different people. Considering a current topic as an example, imagine reading a message suggesting that a particular vaccine is safe and effective. The message might be attributed to a Nobel Prize–winning medical scientist or to a high school student from Arkansas. Either way, it is the same message, just the source is different. What research like this found is that the source often matters, and sometimes the source matters a lot. Messages can be more or less persuasive depending on who people think the source is. People are more likely to be persuaded by a credible source, in this case, the Nobel laureate.

Dimensions

After it was discovered that some sources were more persuasive than others, research turned to investigating what it was about credible sources that made them credible. The features or aspects that comprise perceived believability are called the **dimensions of source credibility**. Different researchers produced different lists and labels, but two common themes emerged. The first dimension might be called **expertise or competence**. This basic idea is that the sources people find credible appear to know what they are talking about. They have special knowledge of or experience with the topic. Winning a Nobel Prize in science, for example, conveys competence and expertise in one's field. Similarly, when Wheeless was able to show his knowledge when answering students' questions, he demonstrated expertise in a way that led me to find him credible. In a restaurant review, expertise can come from experience eating at many different restaurants, as well as knowledge about food and food service.

The second big dimension of credibility is **trustworthiness**. We are more likely to believe people who come off as honest. Together, expertise and trustworthiness are the two most important dimensions of source credibility. To be credible, you need to be seen as having both.

1. Hovland and Weiss (1951).

Building Credibility

In ongoing relationships, credibility can be gradually built over time by demonstrating that you know what you are talking about, that you have your act together, and that you are a reliable, trustworthy person of integrity. Of course, credibility can also be eroded, sometimes quite rapidly, by behaving in ways that undermine credibility. Getting facts wrong, making fallacious arguments, being caught in a lie, or being self-serving to the detriment of others undercut credibility.

There are many paths to gradually establishing credibility in ongoing social, personal, and professional relationships. Here are just a few. Making sound arguments and expressing evidence-based opinions is one approach. Demonstrating competence by successfully completing assigned tasks conveys credibility as well. When you do fail or err, offer a sincere apology to those who are impacted, promise to do better next time, and do not make the same mistake again. Avoid the appearance of conflicts of interest. Communicate as honestly as possible. Show concern and regard for the welfare and the well-being of others. Treat others fairly. Actions such as these build *social capital* and credibility.

In situations where you want to establish credibility more quickly, here are five things you can do. The first is *credentialing*. Make your experience, education, job title, and/or qualifications known to your audience. Second, when you are talking, avoid disfluencies in your delivery. Avoid ums, ahs, likes, and so forth. Third, use relevant evidence if possible, and be sure to provide citations for the evidence. Fourth, avoid appearing self-serving. You want to appear neutral and objective or, even better, to be going against your own self-interest. This will enhance trustworthiness. Finally, be friendly, nice, polite, and respectful. Credibility and likability go together, and impressions of one rub off on the other.

In my work on deception and deception detection, I have found a constellation of behaviors and impressions that tend to be associated with speakers appearing believable. I call this the BQ for **believability quotient**. Be friendly and engaged in the interaction. People tend to believe confident, friendly extroverts, or at least people who come off as such. Second, people who are believed appear confident and composed as opposed to anxious, nervous, uncertain, or ambivalent. Third, communication content needs to sound plausible and reasonable. Finally, the previous three need to be maintained evenly throughout the interaction. The impressions need to come off consistently over time. People who get these facets of their demeanor working together are likely to be believed. They come off as credible.

Moderators

There are at least three moderators of source credibility. Credibility has a greater impact on persuasiveness when audience involvement is low, when the source is identified before rather than after the message is received, and when the message is counter-attitudinal.

The first of these, involvement, works opposite of evidence. Remember from the last chapter that involvement has to do with how much the audience cares about the topic, how important the topic is to them, how central it is to their values, and how much the message might affect them. The basic rule is that the more important the topic is to the audience, the more the message content matters, and the less it matters who the message came from. Thus, when involvement is high, argument quality and evidence are more impactful; when involvement is low, source credibility has a larger impact.

So long as a source is credible, persuasion is boosted when people know who the source is upfront. The source's credibility can rub off on the message. The reverse is true for low-credibility sources. People can dismiss otherwise persuasive messages because they doubt the source.

Finally, source credibility matters more when we disagree with a message. When we already agree, there is less of a boost from high source credibility, and we are more likely to give a low credible source a pass. But, when we disagree, we might give the message more consideration if it comes from a highly credible source, while we will quickly dismiss a low credible source.

The Sleeper Effect

The final subtopic under source credibility is the effect of credibility on the amount of persuasion over time. The persuasive advantages of highly credible sources compared to low credible sources can wear off over time. This is called the **sleeper effect**. Remember how a credibility experiment goes? The audience hears the same persuasive message attributed to one of two sources: one more credible than the other. The typical finding is that people are more persuaded by the highly credible source even though the message is the same. Messages from a credible source get a persuasion boost, while a low credible source undermines the persuasive impact of the message. That is, with a low credible source, the message would have been more persuasive, but for who said it. The message gets dismissed because the source is not believed.

If the researchers tested the persuasion sometime later, the advantage of the highly credible source compared to the low credible source would be less. The persuasiveness of the more credible source would decline over time as people forgot who said it. The persuasive of the less credible source, in contrast, would improve over time as people forgot who said it. People remember the message but not where they heard it or from whom, and thus, it looks like the low credible source is becoming more persuasive as time passes. This is the sleeper effect.

Chapter Summary

- A source is credible when the audience perceives them as believable.
- The two major dimensions of credibility are expertise and trustworthiness.
- Credibility can be enhanced by having good sound communication content, having and citing evidence, avoiding the appearance of conflicts of interest, and by a smooth, friendly, confident delivery.
- The persuasive impact of credibility is maximized immediately after the message is heard, when the audience is less involved when highly credible sources are identified before the message is received, and when the audience disagrees with the message.

Next up, we will continue with the general theme of persuasion and discuss emotional appeals. Dr. Shebib will talk about using emotions to persuade—Aristotle's pathos.

CHAPTER 9

Emotional Appeals

[Dr. Shebib's Voice]

When the coronavirus entered the United States in February 2020, I was working on my dissertation, as I was expected to graduate with my doctorate degree in May 2020. I remember the day vividly. I was in a suburb of Detroit, Michigan, an epicenter of COVID-19. Classes were just about to resume from spring break, but MSU was forced to shut down as the coronavirus pandemic was hitting us hard. Persuasive emotional appeals were everywhere (as they normally are), but this was especially true during the COVID-19 pandemic. Fear appeals, in particular, were a commonplace tactic during the pandemic, but they had a long history of use in health campaigns prior to the pandemic. When COVID hit the United States in early March of 2020, fear was the main reason people quickly adopted wearing face masks, began being diligent about washing hands for at least 20 seconds, and stayed quarantined. What I find particularly interesting, however, is how, over time, people's philosophies on these matters shifted. Yes, there's a good portion of people who are still complying with these recommendations from health-care officials, but there are also other people who stopped complying with pandemic best practices. This is so intriguing to me because this is not a situation that has just an effect on one person. People are unilaterally behaving in ways that affect others around them. If I don't take preventative measures to reduce my chances of contracting COVID-19, my students, colleagues, family, 92-year-old grandparents, and people who I've been in the presence of (even if I don't know them) are at a higher risk of contracting it. My behavior is literally affecting the health of other people and vice versa, and in some situations, it's a life-or-death matter.

Maybe health-care professionals scared some people too much? Maybe some people think that they are at less risk compared to other Americans? Well, this is actually true. People do think they are at less risk than other people when it comes to negative consequences of health decisions (more on this later). Or maybe people just got tired of worrying about it? Whatever the case might be, the health messaging during the pandemic highlights how fear appeals can be effective and ineffective at the same time (even regarding the same fear-appealing message). It also shows how people experience emotions differently, and how they act upon those emotions isn't always in line with the recommended action.

Pathos

Pathos is persuasion that appeals to the audience's emotions. Examples of pathos can be seen in everything from classical essays to contemporary advertisements. Language choice and nonverbal communication codes (such as vocalics; see Chapter 14) affect the audience's emotional response, and emotional appeals can, when used competently, enhance the power of an argument. Emotions are generally viewed as involving an internal affective state (e.g., mood)[1] and specific feeling states[2] that vary in terms of intensity.[3] When we experience an emotion, it is generally short-lived, but it can be intense and directed at some stimuli. The emotional state of the audience can be incredibly powerful in aiding or hindering the process of persuasion.

An appeal to pathos can allow the audience members to understand the persuader's point of view in a more visually meaningful way. **Emotional appeals strategically and intentionally aim to evoke an emotion to help facilitate the persuasive message.** However, emotional appeals can induce different intensities of emotional states, in addition to different emotions. Thus, the keys to persuasive effectiveness are the proper identification of the emotion, knowing the action tendencies (i.e., how people typically respond) associated with different emotions, and having a way for the prompted emotion to facilitate the persuasive goals. For example, if we want to use fear to scare someone into a healthy behavior, we want to scare them just the right amount in a way that reduces their fear and prompts them to make a healthy choice rather than "running away" from the problem.

Types of Emotional Appeals

Persuaders use different types of emotional appeals to persuade others. Typically, the types of emotions used are classified as positive or negative emotions. It is important to note that sometimes, we experience both types of emotions through a singular persuasive message. However, research has found that emotions contain multiple components because they affect our physiology, cognition, and action tendencies.

Positive emotions (e.g., happiness, compassion, hope) refer to pleasant and desirable affective moods. Physiologically, positive emotions are associated with increased skin temperature, decreased cortisol (i.e., the "stress" hormone), and lowered heart rates. In terms of cognition, when we experience positive emotions, we are more likely to process persuasive messages through peripheral routes and heuristic processing (less effortful and less mindful cognition). Thus, we are less likely to scrutinize information and more likely to base judgments on simplified knowledge structures. Finally, the action tendencies associated with positive emotions are usually passive. For example, when we feel happiness, we have action tendencies of contentment and relaxation. Thus, **positive emotional appeals have been found to increase positive thoughts through positive associations but can make a target less motivated to act on the issue at hand, but it can also facilitate approach behaviors[4] and continued action.**[5]

Negative emotions (e.g., fear, guilt, anger, sadness) refer to unpleasant and undesirable affective states. Physiologically, negative emotions are associated with decreased skin temperature, increased cortisol, and elevated heart rates. Regarding cognition, when we experience negative emotions, we are more likely to process persuasive messages through a central route and systematic processing. That is, we are more likely to scrutinize information and less likely to base judgments on simplified knowledge. Finally, the action tendencies associated with negative emotions are usually proactive. For example, when we experience anger, we have the action tendency to retaliate and subdue the offending stimulus. Thus, negative emotional appeals can be incredibly powerful at drawing attention to a persuasive message. On the other hand, negative emotional appeals can

1. Forgas (1995).

2. For example, anger, happiness; Ekman (2003).

3. Dillard and Pfau (2002).

4. Cacioppo et al. (1999), Watson et al. (1999).

5. Carver and Scheier (1990).

provoke impulsive reactions, and backlash can also occur. If the target perceives the negative emotional appeal message as manipulative, it can prompt a reactance in the target, and a boomerang effect (i.e., opposite outcome than intended) can unfold. **Negative emotional appeals have been found to be risky to associate with but more motivating for audience members to act upon.**

Fear Appeals

Fear appeals are the most studied emotional appeal in persuasion research. The idea is to convince the audience that they are at risk and provide them with a path to safety. Kim Witte[6] defines *fear appeals* as messages that *"cause fear focusing on the severity and probability of occurrence of a threat to induce the adherence to a recommended action."* There has been much research on fear appeals, and we have a wealth of information regarding the psychology of fear and the influence fear appeals have on the persuasion process. Most of this research has been devoted to examining fear-arousing health messages that aim at convincing people to alter unhealthy habits and adopt healthy ones (e.g., wearing face masks, vaping, unsafe sex, drunk driving, texting and driving, indoor tanning).

So, when do fear appeals work best?

In the protection motivation approach,[7] there are three necessary components of an effective fear appeal: severity, certainty, and options. *Severity* involves the terrible thing that could happen to you if you do not follow the advice of the message. The worse the potentially bad thing described, the greater the severity. *Certainty* communicates that the bad thing could happen to you. The greater the certainty, the more likely the bad thing is to happen if you do nothing to prevent it. Finally, *options* refer to what you need to do to prevent the scary bad thing. These days, options are usually called **efficacy**. Having efficacy means that you can feel in control. Putting efficacy in a persuasive message involves trying to empower the audience by giving them a solution to avoid the risk depicted in the message. The idea is that without a scary bad thing that might happen to you to make you afraid and without a way to avoid the fear, a fear appeal will not be persuasive.

Boster and Mongeau[8] found that high fear messages (high in severity) tend to work better on older rather than younger audiences. They also found that scary persuasive messages worked better when people encountered them voluntarily and with people lower in anxiety.

Many approaches to persuasion are known as dual-process models.[9] Dual-process models suggest that there are two paths to persuasion: a thoughtful, reasoned path (sometimes called central or systematic processing) and a more mindless, automatic path with simple decision rules (sometimes called the peripheral and heuristic approach). One of these dual-process models, known as the *stage model*,[10] helps illuminate how the intensity of fear works. According to the model, when a person is exposed to a fear-arousing message, the person engages in *threat appraisal to* assess the *perceived severity* of the threat and her or his *perceived vulnerability* to the threat. If both severity and vulnerability are seen as low, a person will tend to ignore the threat or rely on peripheral processing. If only severity is high and vulnerability is low, the person will engage in moderate cognitive processing. When perceived severity and perceived vulnerability are both high, defense motivation kicks in, and the person uses

6. Witte (1994).

7. Rogers and Prentice-Dunn (1997).

8. Boster and Mongeau (1984).

9. Petty and Cacioppo (1986a, 1986b).

10. de Hoog et al. (2007, 2008).

central processing. Under defense motivation, a person actively scrutinizes the message and evaluates strategies for minimizing the harm.

How do people respond to these threats?

The *extended parallel process model* (EPPM) *of fear appeals*[11] suggests that people who are exposed to a fear-arousing message can respond in one of two ways. First, they could act by perceiving they are at risk, so they avoid the danger (referred to as *danger control*). This is what the persuader wants. Second, they could be fixated on reducing their fear without reducing their risk. (This second possibility is referred to as *fear control*, and it might involve a rationalization such as it will not happen to me, or it will not be that bad). In EPPM, danger control is a far more effective response because it focuses on the solution. Fear control, conversely, is counterproductive because it focuses on managing one's fear. A persuader's goal in using fear appeals, then, should be to arouse fear in a manner that triggers danger control rather than fear control.

Important Implications

It would seem like scaring people into healthy behaviors should be easy. All you must do is invoke terrifying outcomes and then sit back, as fear should manifest to people to change their behavior. But it's not that easy. And there are two important misconceptions I must mention as to why. The first questionable assumption is that fear appeals usually work, and second, fear may act as a simple drive. However, fear appeals are not always effective because (1) it's hard to manipulate fear; (2) if you scare someone too much, it can backfire (causing a boomerang effect)[12]; and (3) the *illusion of invulnerability*,[13] which is the belief that one is less likely to experience negative events in life than other people.

Chapter Summary

- Emotional appeals affect the recipient's physiology, cognition, and response tendencies.
- Positive emotional appeals have been found to increase positive thoughts through positive associations but can make a target less motivated to act.
- Negative emotions have been found to be risky to associate with but more motivating for audience members to act upon.

Next up, I will discuss Cialdini's weapons of influence!

11. Witte et al. (1996).

12. Morris and Swann (1996).

13. Weinstein (1980, 1993).

CHAPTER 10

Cialdini's Weapons of Influence

[*Dr. Shebib's Voice*]

Robert Cialdini is the Regents' Professor Emeritus of Psychology and Marketing at Arizona State University (ASU), where I had the honor to learn from him when I attended ASU for my undergraduate degree. He's known to many as the "godfather of persuasion." He is a *New York Times* best-selling author and renowned social scientist. Dr. Cialdini's books are published in 44 languages and have sold over 7 million copies.

What I remember most about Dr. Cialdini's class are (1) how an old palm reader's trick can leverage to get people to do what you want; (2) why persuasion does not just depend on the message itself but also on how the message is presented; (3) what research reveals about why the context matters as much, if not more, than the content itself; (4) why you shouldn't ask people for their opinion but instead ask someone for advice; and, finally, (5) how small differences that seem trivial can make a huge impact on human behavior.

When I think about Dr. Cialdini's weapons of influence, the first thing that comes to mind is their simplicity. These aren't overly complicated ways to influence other people. They are all quite simple. However, the evidence and research behind them are voluminous, and their impact is powerful. What is more, these can be applied to almost every persuasive situation you can think of. From sales to marketing to influence on social media, these seven principles provide the forces behind the most effective strategies for influencing people. In this chapter, I will discuss what the weapons of influence are and provide an overview of his seven principles and the research to back them up. This way, you can learn from Dr. Cialdini too.

Cialdini's Weapons of Influence

Over 60 years of research have been devoted to understanding the factors that influence people to say "yes." When deciding to buy something or do something, it would be nice to think that people consider all available information and make a rational decision. However, that's just not always the case. Instead, we tend to use mental shortcuts or rule-of-thumbs to guide the decisions we make. Mental shortcuts are sometimes called **heuristics**. Cialdini (2021)[1] refers to these universal shortcuts that guide our behavior as **weapons of influence**. His research, combined with other social scientists, has identified seven that are especially important in persuasion. These include reciprocity, liking, social proof, authority, scarcity, commitment and consistency, and unity.

---

1. The content from this chapter comes from Cialdini (2021) and other research.

Reciprocity

The rule of **reciprocity** states that we should try to repay or return in kind what someone has provided for us. If someone does us a favor, we should do one for them in return. If someone posts an Instagram story for our birthday, we should remember their birthday and post one for them as well. We feel *obligated* to repay others for what they have done or given for us.

An impressive aspect of reciprocation with its accompanying sense of obligation is its pervasiveness across human cultures. Research has found all human societies subscribe to the rule, although there are some cultures where it is especially strong. This is called **the norm of reciprocity**.[2]

Cialdini describes several ways reciprocity occurs in interactions. The first general technique is referred to as "*the give and take*." I give you something, and in return, I take something from you that you've given to me. As a marketing technique, the "free" sample strategy engages the reciprocity rule. Accepting a free sample can trigger the natural indebting force that is inherent in receiving a gift. For example, retail giant Costco offers free samples of a variety of products they sell. Interestingly, almost all the cost of the free samples is covered by shoppers who end up purchasing the product.[3] Additionally, trying products at home for free is another persuasive technique that engages the rule of reciprocity because it leads people to purchase them.

Another example is waiters giving a mint to customers in a restaurant at the end of service. Giving the mint at the end of a meal typically increased tips by 3%. If the gift is doubled and two mints are provided, tips don't double; they quadruple—a 14% increase in tips. Most interestingly, when a waiter puts one mint on the table, starts to walk away, but pauses, turns back, and hands extra mints, tips go through the roof—a 23% increase in the tip![4]

Finally, there is the *door-in-the-face* technique. In this technique, you first want to make a large request of someone. A large request, you know, is most likely to be turned down. Then, after it is turned down, offer a second and smaller request—this should be the request you wanted all along (see Chapter 11 for more on this).

Liking

The next weapon of influence is **liking**. People prefer to say "yes" to individuals they like. Cialdini reports several factors that can increase one's likability. First is physical attractiveness. Physical attractiveness is accompanied by a *halo effect*,[5] which means that people we perceive as physically attractive also reap the benefits of being perceived as having other positive characteristics, such as credibility and intelligence. As a result, physically attractive people are more persuasive.

Similarity is a second factor. We like people who are like us, and we are more willing to say yes to their requests. Another factor is *praise*. Compliments usually enhance liking and compliance. *Increased familiarity* through repeated contact is another factor that can contribute to liking. Finally, there is *association*. Positive associations with brands, companies, and things alike can simply enhance compliance. For example, people who have positive associations with Apple are more likely to have an iPhone and other Apple products compared to other brands. People (sports fans, for example) try to associate with favorable events and distance themselves from unfavorable ones.

2. Gouldner (1960).

3. Cialdini (2021).

4. Strohmetz et al. (2002).

5. Dion et al. (1972; i.e., the "what is beautiful is good hypothesis").

Social Proof

The principle of **social proof** states that one important means people use to decide what to believe or how to act in a situation is to examine what other people are doing or believing. It is the principle behind *conformity* and *"bandwagon."* It relies on *normative influence*. Both children and adults are affected. The principle of social proof can be used to stimulate a person's compliance with a request by communicating that many people (the more, the better) are or have been complying with it. Therefore, simply pointing to the popularity of an item elevates the item's popularity. The appearance of popularity can also be created, for example, by bars letting people in slowly so that there is a longer line to get in than necessary.

Cialdini states that social proof is most effective under three conditions. The first is *uncertainty*: When we are unsure, we are more likely to be influenced by other people. The second condition is *"the many"*: The more people involved, the more someone will feel inclined to follow suit. The third condition is *similarity*: People conform to people they perceive are like themselves. "Viral marketing" is based on this. Malcolm Gladwell[6] argued that in the same way, a sick person can start an epidemic of the flu (or COVID-19, too soon?), so too can a small group of influential people launch a fashion trend or boost the popularity of a new product. The idea is that consumers will see products being used or talked about by others and follow suit.

Social proof, of course, has the power to influence more than buying behavior, as illustrated in a study.[7] Researchers posted two signs near elevators. One, using social proof, read, "More than 90 percent of the time, people in this building use the stairs instead of the elevator." The other sign said, "Taking the stairs instead of the elevator is a good way to get some exercise." Within 2 weeks, the number of people using the elevator instead of the stairs dropped 46%, but only in the social proof condition. No change was observed with the sign that merely encouraged exercise.

Authority

In the 1960s, Stanley Milgram,[8] a professor from Yale University, conducted a series of experiments on the power of authority. Participants who were assigned the teacher role were repeatedly ordered by a researcher to deliver increasingly intense and apparently dangerous levels of shock to a learner simply because they were instructed to do so by an authority figure. However, what participants were not aware of was that the learner was a paid actor, and the shocks they were administering were not real. Even though the learner would cry out in agony, begging the teacher to stop administering the shocks, results from the Milgram study found that 65% of the participants continued administering the shocks all the way up to 450 bolts, at which point the researcher concluded the experiment.

The Milgram study demonstrates the strong pressures for compliance when an authority issues a request. Further, people even tend to obey mere symbols of authority. These symbols consist of titles (e.g., doctor), clothing (e.g., police or military uniform), and trappings, such as automobiles, and they are powerful nonverbal elements that communicate authority, which influences our obedience to comply with that person.

6. Gladwell (2002).

7. Burger and Shelton (2011).

8. Milgram (1963).

Scarcity

According to the **scarcity** principle, people assign more value to opportunities and things that are less available. The use of this principle for profit can be seen in such compliance techniques known as *deadline tactics*—the "limited-time" offer wherein people try to convince us that if we don't, we will lose something of value. This engages the human tendency for **loss aversion**—people are more motivated by the thought of losing something than by the thought of gaining something of equal value.

Scarcity is a principle that savvy retailers are using more and more with success. Streetwear retailers such as Supreme popularized the concept of the product "drop." Less product than demand causes limited edition drops to sell out in minutes.

According to Cialdini and other researchers, people love freedom, and when that freedom is threatened or limited, people experience something called **psychological reactance**, which is a perceived loss or threat to free behavior. When we experience psychological reactance, we can react psychologically by desiring something more than we actually desire it. People also attempt to use psychological reactance in their favor by making time scarce. For instance, by telling us that we must "act now" or that there is a "limited-time offer," advertisers are relying on the principle of scarcity. By limiting our time, they hope it makes us more likely to purchase their product or service. At the same time, reactance can make persuasion backfire if people feel too pressured.

Commitment and Consistency

The desire for consistency comes down to wanting to align our external behaviors with our inner beliefs and values. As humans, we don't like to appear inconsistent. No one wants to be the person who goes back on their word. When you get someone to commit verbally to an action, the chances of them completing that action go up drastically. It is important to understand that the power of commitment and consistency does not come just because someone says so. It is driven out of their emotions and values. Even if the original incentive or motivation is removed after they have already agreed, they will continue to honor the agreement. For example, in car sales, suddenly raising the price at the last moment works because the buyer has already decided to buy. Additionally, marketers make you close popups on their website by saying, "I'll sign up later." Some other approaches that are based on the principle of consistency and commitment are low-balling and foot-in-the-door strategies (see Chapter 11 for more details).

Unity

The newest weapon of influence by Cialdini is that of **unity** ("we-ness"). People are more likely to say "yes" or be persuaded by someone they consider one of them. Although unity, on the surface, may sound similar to liking, unity moves beyond surface-level similarities as it is about shared identities. In a way, unity fulfills a third step in Maslow's[9] hierarchy of needs: the need to belong. When we belong or feel we belong to a group, we're likely to be more open to persuasion attempts.

---

9. Maslow (1943, 1954).

Chapter Summary

- Weapons of influence are universal shortcuts that guide human behavior.
- The seven weapons of influence are reciprocity, liking, social proof, authority, scarcity, commitment and consistency, and unity.

In the next chapter, Dr. Levine will discuss compliance-gaining strategies.

CHAPTER 11

Compliance-Gaining Strategies

[*Dr. Levine's Voice*]

In the mid-1970s, Gerald R. Miller (from the previous chapter on the three types of questions) taught a doctoral seminar at Michigan State based on his latest book, *Between People*. The book outlined a new approach to interpersonal communication, and it became one of the most influential works on the topic. Miller was still using the book in 1987 when I took graduate interpersonal communication from him. To this day, I use Miller's framework when I teach interpersonal communication, although his book is long out of print. It forever changed my understanding of communication.

Anyway, students in his seminar split into two groups, forming two research teams investigating ideas from the book. One team studied deception, doing a study that influenced the subsequent McCornack and Park's model of relational deception and eventually truth-default theory (see Chapter 25). The other team studied the topic of this chapter, compliance gaining. Miller and three then-students published an article that is now known as "MBRS."[1] MBRS was the first communication study on the topic of compliance gaining, and it got the ball rolling, so to speak.

Following MBRS, the early compliance-gaining research in communication tended to focus on two basic questions. First, what are the message options for people to get someone to do something for you? That is, what are the types or categories of compliance-gaining strategies? Second, under what conditions will people use one type of strategy over another? Much research ensued, but by the mid-1990s, enthusiasm had waned. Scholars argued over who had the best list of strategies. As it turns out, people usually stick with just a couple of simple message strategies: direct requests and direct requests with reasons.

At the same time, more interesting compliance-gaining research was going on in social psychology, most notably by Robert Cialdini, whom Dr. Shebib covered in Chapter 10. This research typically involved field experiments, and it focused on testing the effectiveness of specific strategies and understanding why they worked. Over time, Frank Boster (from MBRS) and his students (e.g., me, Chris Carpenter, and many others) moved away from the old communication questions and shifted our focus to message effectiveness. My PhD dissertation, for example, not only looked at what strategies people used but also at what worked.[2] It has been decades since I published a compliance-gaining study, but it was my research specialty before I shifted to deception. The opportunity to study under Miller and Boster was why I chose to do my PhD at Michigan State. Compliance gaining is still one of my favorite topics. I have been looking forward to writing this chapter.

1. Pronounced eM-BeRS, for the authors: Gerald Miller, Frank Boster, Michael Roloff, and David Seibold; Miller et al. (1977).
2. Levine and Boster (2001).

What Is Compliance Gaining?

Compliance gaining is a type of *social influence* (how humans influence other humans). It involves *getting someone to do something through verbal messages*. The focus is on *behavioral outcomes*. Do me this favor. Donate to this cause. It is different from *persuasion* in that persuasion often seeks to change people's internal psychological states like their opinions, attitudes, or beliefs. Persuasion aims to obtain *private acceptance* or "buy-in." If I am trying to get you to believe that vaccines are safe or that being vaccinated is a good thing, that is persuasion. If I just want to get a shot, and that is the bottom line, that is compliance gaining. Following the speed limit is an issue of compliance; accepting that speed limits should be followed is an issue of persuasion.

Everyday Compliance Gaining

As we will see as this chapter progresses, if you want to get someone to do something, there are a wide variety of strategies you might choose from. Some work better than others, and some only work under certain conditions. But if you just observe people and watch what they do in their normal lives, most instances of compliance gaining involve one of two flexible, widely applicable, and simple approaches.

One of the things people do most often is a **direct request**. They just ask. "Hey, could you give me a ride to the airport?" Often, direct requests are phrased politely. "Could you give me a ride, *please*?" "If it is not too much trouble, could you give me a ride?" "I hate to ask, but could you loan me a few dollars?" Nevertheless, regardless of the polite packaging, these all involve just asking.

Typically, research on compliance gaining uses direct requests as the control group. The question is, can we do better than a simple request? But we should not be critical of polite requests. Remember, if you do not ask, you will not get, and being polite is better than being rude.

Interestingly, when compliance-gaining strategies fail, and the target of the messages does not comply, people typically do not shift to another strategy. In one of my favorite findings ever, Professor Charles Berger found that when thwarted in their goals, communicators often just say the same thing again, only louder.[3]

The other thing people often do is make a direct request plus a **reason**. "Could you give me a ride to the airport *because* parking is expensive, and I am going to be gone for several days? It would save me a lot of money." Of course, these too are often dressed up in politeness.

The Power of Providing a Reason

One of my favorite experiments is by psychologist Ellen Langer.[4] It took place back in the days of copy machines at libraries. It went like this. People asked people waiting in line to cut in front of them. Some of the time, they made a small request of only 5 pages, sometimes a bigger request of 20 pages. They phrased the request in one of three ways:

1. "Excuse me, I have 5 (or 20) pages. May I use the Xerox machine?"

---

3. Berger and di Battista (2009).

4. Langer et al. (1978).

2. "Excuse me, I have 5 (or 20) pages. May I use the Xerox machine *because* I have to make copies?"
3. "Excuse me, I have 5 (or 20) pages. May I use the Xerox machine *because I'm in a rush?*"

Message (1) is a direct request. Messages (2) and (3) are different versions of a request plus a reason. Message (2), however, is really a pseudo-reason. It has the structure of a reason because it includes the word "because." The content of the reason, however, is vacuous. It is circular. Message (3), in contrast, offers a real reason. Thus, the experiment tests the power of adding a reason to a direct request and if the reason needs to be a good one.

Here are the results. For small requests, the percentage of people agreeing to the three requests was 60%, 93%, and 94%, respectively. The simple presence of "because" (the superficial impression of giving a reason) improved compliance. The pattern was different for the larger request of 20 pages. The rates were 24%, 24%, and 42%. The rates were lower overall because it was a bigger request. This time, the validity of the reason mattered. Having a good reason always worked better. If people were not listening carefully, even the appearance of a reason helped.

Sequential Request Strategies

The other specific compliance-gaining strategies that we will cover fall under the label of sequential request strategies. What makes them sequential is that they all have multiple steps that need to be done in a particular order. For each of them, you will want to know the name of the strategy, its definition, what are the steps involved, the order of the steps, why it works, and the conditions under which it works. The reason why a strategy works is called the *mechanism*. Often, the mechanism is one of Cialdini's principles discussed in the previous chapter. The conditions under which a strategy is effective are called *moderators*.

The first sequential request strategy was the **foot-in-the-door** (FITD) strategy.[5] The FITD involves asking a small request, getting compliance, and then asking a larger real request. For example, someone might ask you to sign a petition in support of some worthy cause. Once you sign, they then ask for a donation. The idea is you are more likely to donate if you previously signed the petition. The mechanism is consistency. The key moderator is that it only works for prosocial requests (i.e., good causes).[6]

Cialdini identified a second strategy known as **door-in-the-face** (DITF).[7] DITF is also known as *reciprocal concessions* or *reject-and-retreat*. It is the opposite order of the FITD. You make a big request first, one that is sure to be rejected, and then, once rejected, you make a smaller request, which is what you really wanted all along. "Can I borrow $1,000?" "No." "How about $50 then?" It works because of reciprocation. You create the illusion of compromise. Research has indicated that it has several moderators.[8] Like FITD, it only works for prosocial requests. Unlike FITD, it also requires that the same person make both requests and that the second request follows immediately (no time delay) after the first request.

Cialdini's next strategy was "**even a penny helps**," also called *legitimizing paltry contributions*.[9] This strategy

5. Freedman and Fraser (1966).
6. Dillard et al. (1984).
7. Cialdini et al. (1975).
8. Feeley et al. (2012) and O'Keefe and Hale (2009).
9. Cialdini and Schroeder (1976).

is just like it sounds. You make a request for a donation and then add "even a penny helps" at the end. Cialdini found that it increased both the chances that someone would donate and the amount donated. The strategy makes it harder to say no.

A related strategy is "**but you are free**" (BYAF).[10] Instead of saying even a penny, you say, but you are free to say no at the end. It overcomes resistance by seeming to be a low-pressure request. It counteracts the *psychological reactance* that was discussed in the last chapter under Cialdini's principle of scarcity.

In 1978, Cialdini published the **low-ball strategy**. We can also call this *bait-and-switch*. In the low ball, an incentive is offered for compliance, and once the person agrees, the incentive is withdrawn. This strategy is sometimes used in car sales. A salesperson offers a great deal, the customer agrees, and the salesperson reveals that the deal is not as good as it seemed. Like FITD, it works because of consistency. Unlike FITD and DITF, its effectiveness is not limited to prosocial requests.

Next up is the **that's-not-all** (TNA) strategy.[11] TNA is a mainstay of television infomercials and product commercials. The sequence is that an offer is made, and time passes, but before the person can respond, the deal is sweetened. It can work in two ways. First, a bonus can be added. That's not all; we will throw in this other thing too. Or it can work as a discount. If you buy now, we will lower the price by $10. TNA works because of reciprocation and by creating a favorable contrast or comparison.

The **pregiving** strategy involves doing someone a favor or giving someone a gift before making a request.[12] It appears to work because it enhances liking.[13]

The most useful sequential strategy is **dump-and-chase**.[14] I call this strategy *overcoming objections*. We have already noted that when people make a direct request, sometimes they provide a reason. It is also the case that when people turn down a request, they often provide a reason. In dump-and-chase, the reasons for noncompliance are anticipated and overcome. Dump-and-chase begins with a direct request. If the person complies, great. Compliance has been gained. If the person says no and offers a reason, the reason is countered. The compliance seeker will have planned ways to overcome each potential reason for noncompliance, and they keep countering the reasons as long as reasons are offered. If the person does not give a reason, they are politely asked for one. Dump-and-chase makes it hard to say no. It couples the power of providing reasons with persistence wearing down the target. Here is an example:

> Person 1: Would you care to donate to the American Cancer Society?
>
> Person 2: No
>
> Person 1: May I ask why not?
>
> Person 2: I don't have any money on me.
>
> Person 1: We take credit cards.

10. Carpenter (2012).

11. Burger (1986).

12. Regan (1971).

13. Goei et al. (2003).

14. Boster et al. (2009).

The last strategy is **disrupt-then-reframe**.[15] The disrupt part is saying something odd or confusing. Then you make the request along with a reason. It works by reducing resistance. The target is thrown off by the initial confusing statement. You want to buy these cookies? They cost 150 pennies, that's $1.50, they are yummy.

Chapter Summary

- Compliance gaining involves getting other people to do things.
- Direct requests and direct requests plus reasons are the most common ways people try to gain compliance.
- Sequential request strategies all involve multiple parts done in a specific order. They can be more effective than direct requests.

Next up, Dr. Shebib will discuss the role of the audience in persuasion.

15. Davis and Knowles (1999).

CHAPTER 12

The Audience

[Dr. Shebib's Voice]

T he number one rule in persuasion is to know your audience and adapt to them! This sounds simple, but it can be harder than you might think. For one thing, sometimes you don't have much information about your audience members. Even so, get as much information as possible on your audience before persuading them. That way, you can adjust your strategy accordingly! Additionally, when speaking, nonverbal communication (discussed more in Chapter 14) from audience members can communicate a host of information regarding people's viewpoints and how they are reacting to you. Reading people's expressions, in addition to knowing your audience, will help you become more effective at persuasion. I do this every time I teach. I'm constantly reading facial expressions to see if students are understanding what I am saying or if I need to explain something in more depth. Remember, you must adapt to be effective. This also ties into a concept we will discuss in the final chapter of this book: communication competence. **Knowing what is effective and appropriate requires knowing your audience!**

Conformity

Solomon Asch[1] conducted an experiment to investigate the extent to which social pressure from a majority group could affect a person to conform. Asch conducted a "vision test" lab experiment, where participants were asked to match the lengths of lines. Each participant performed the task in a room with seven other confederates (i.e., people who were part of the experiment but who the participant thought were other participants). The confederates had agreed in advance what their response would be when presented with the line task. Each person in the room was asked to state aloud which comparison line was the same length as the target line. The answer was always obvious. Sometimes, the confederates all gave the same wrong answer. The real participant sat at the end of the row and would give his answer second to last. Asch measured the number of times each participant conformed to the majority view when the majority was incorrect. On average, participants who were placed in this situation went along and conformed with the clearly incorrect majority on about one third (32%) of the critical trials.

The Asch experiment is understood as showing the power of conformity, which, of course, it does. But a careful look at the results shows something else too. On average, people conformed about a third of the time. However, there were people who always conformed, people who never conformed, and people everywhere

1. Asch (1956).

in between. Some people were more susceptible to normative influence than others! It follows that using a normative appeal will work better on some people than others.

A more recent example of conformity comes from an experiment[2] where the researchers sent out household home electricity reports to a group of randomized homes. These reports, referred to as nudges, provided energy-saving tips as well as information on electricity usage relative to their neighbors. The control group received no reports. At first glance, the results made it appear that the nudges worked well and saved energy. However, further analyses revealed a significant qualification. Political liberals reduced consumption, on average, by 3%. But conservatives increased consumption, on average, by 1%. Nudging backfired with those who identified as conservatives. Apparently, the nudges angered some of the target audience, and they did the reverse of what was requested. Consequently, persuasive effectiveness could be maximized by more selective targeting. **In communication, one size does not fit all, and a good communicator adapts their message based on their audience.**

Mere Exposure

One way people differ from others is in what they have previously been exposed to. **Mere exposure** is a concept by Robert Zajonc.[3] It is defined as when *repeated exposure to a stimulus enhances a person's attitude toward the stimulus.* This is different from repetition, which helps you remember things. For example, when studying for an exam, you want to read over your notes several times. Mere exposure isn't like studying. It is passive and can be as simple as passing by something in the environment. Your attitude changes depending on whether it is the first time you have seen it or the tenth time. The more you are exposed to something, the more you tend to like it. However, that is up to a point. For example, seeing the McDonald's sign isn't going to affect you after seeing it 25 or more times. Does your audience have prior exposure to you? If they don't, enhance your exposure.

A meta-analysis[4] showed that the mere exposure effect is robust and a reliable finding. It is strongest with brief exposures in a heterogeneous (i.e., in a mixed-up order) exposure sequence. The mere exposure effect typically levels off after 10 to 20 exposures. Mere exposure, however, does not work for young children. It can even have a reverse effect on children who prefer novel stimuli. There is a stronger effect when the stimulus is complex. And the cool part about it is that you do not even have to be aware that you are being exposed. The subliminal aspect of it makes it hidden but effective.

There is another concept referred to as **mere thought**.[5] *Merely thinking about something polarizes our opinions.* If I get you thinking about something, your opinion tends to grow stronger and more extreme. Mere exposure enhances attitudes. Mere thought polarizes attitudes.

Involvement

Each audience member has a level of involvement regarding the topic you're discussing. Involvement means how

2. Costa and Kahn (2010).

3. Zajonc (1968).

4. Bornstein (1989).

5. Tesser (1978).

relevant or important the topic is to a particular audience member. There are three types of involvement.[6] The first, *value-relevant involvement*, applies to the topics close to your strongly held attitudes, values, and opinions. For example, if someone is discussing addiction or mental health, my ears pop up. Addiction and mental health are important topics to me because I've been directly affected by them, as you'll learn throughout my classes. However, if the topic was regarding fishing, my ears wouldn't pop up. The more value-relevant the topic is to the audience member, the harder it is to persuade them to change their minds. The second type, *outcome-relevant involvement*, addresses the question of how does this affect or impact me? The more an outcome directly affects the audience member, the more you can persuade them with strong arguments and good evidence. Finally, *impression-relevant involvement* affects your image. Holding an opinion that is perceived as more socially acceptable is an example. People who think others will scrutinize their views tend to advocate a more moderate stance on the issue that is seen as more socially appropriate.

Discrepancy

Discrepancy refers to the difference between the view advocated and the view held by the receiver. A low discrepancy message would imply that the view I'm persuading you on is a view similar to what you already hold. Think of the saying "preaching to the choir"—that's low discrepancy. High discrepancy is the opposite—I'm persuading you on something you hold an opposite opinion on. For example, preaching to Donald Trump supporters about the virtues of Elizabeth Warren is high discrepancy. Social judgment theory[7] suggests there's a sweet spot in discrepancy. If the discrepancy is too high, it's an automatic rejection. But if there's just the right amount of discrepancy, you can adapt your persuasive message to the audience member's latitude of acceptance, thereby making it more acceptable to them.

Reactance

Reactance,[8] which was also mentioned in Chapter 10 as psychological reactance, is based on the idea that when people feel pressured into doing something, they will sometimes do the opposite. It refers to the tendency to react defensively to perceived violations of our freedom. People want to make their own decisions. If the audience feels like you're forcing persuasion on them, they will experience reactance. Maybe this is why the nudges didn't work in the previous example. Too much fear in a fear appeal can also produce this. This is a huge reason that a lot of antidrug campaigns are not successful.

There are two types of reactance: (1) *backlash*, which is a perceived threat to one's freedom that produces a defensive reaction, and (2) *forbidden fruit*, which refers to when outlawing or banning something makes it more attractive. For example, a pushy sales clerk might drive customers away, or a parent who criticizes a daughter's boyfriend may drive the daughter into the boyfriend's arms (see Chapter 21). Finally, it's important to mention that there are some individual differences that potentially lead people to be more reactant than others. Some people are just more prone to reactance than others.

6. Johnson and Eagly (1989).
7. Sherif and Hovland (1961).
8. Brehm (1966).

Need for Cognition

Need for cognition[9] is a term for how much people like to think about things. People who are highly in need of cognition are analytical. They are influenced more by the quality of evidence and arguments made. Thus, they respond to persuasive messages best when arguments are cogent and backed up with compelling evidence (see Chapters 6 and 7). They will scrutinize and reflect carefully on the arguments made, and to the extent that their thoughts about the message are favorable, they will modify their attitude in accordance with the message. People low in need for cognition lack the motivation to engage in effortful processing of information. People low in need for cognition rely more on heuristic cues (see Chapter 10), such as the expertise of the communicator (see Chapter 8), to help them decide whether to agree or disagree with a persuasive message.

Dogmatism

Dogmatism[10] is a concept that reflects the opposite of openness (see Chapter 22). People who are high in dogmatism tend to see the world as this way or that way. There is little gray area. One of those ways is the "right" way, and the other is the "wrong" way. For example, dogmatic thinking might label people as liberal or conservative. You couldn't be an independent or moderate. And if you're not what I am, then you're wrong. That's the dogmatic viewpoint. Highly dogmatic individuals tend to view the world as hostile and threatening. They also tend to be into power and control. Conversely, low dogmatic individuals are the opposite; they tend to have a more positive view of the world, and they are not as keen on authority. In terms of persuasion, highly dogmatic individuals are persuaded more by message source (Chapter 8) than message content (Chapters 6 and 7). They are also more unwilling to compromise (see Chapter 24) and use "tell and threat" strategies.

Chapter Summary

- Know your audience and adapt to them!
- Nothing works on everyone.
- Highly value-relevant involved audience members are harder to persuade to an opposing viewpoint.
- Mere exposure enhances attitudes, whereas mere thought polarizes attitudes.
- Moderate discrepancy between your position and audience, in addition to low reactance, is more optimal for successful persuasion.

In the next chapter, Dr. Levine will discuss diffusion of innovation.

9. Cacioppo and Petty (1982).
10. Rokeach (1960).

Diffusion of Innovations

[*Dr. Levine's Voice*]

Back in the day, I wrote my MA thesis by hand on notebook paper, and I hired a typist for the final version. By the time I wrote my doctoral dissertation, I had a personal computer and used word processing software, much like I am writing this chapter. For a dyslexic like me, automated spell check and the ability to edit online have been big, maybe even life-changing, improvements. Writing a book like this would have been much more difficult and time-consuming before personal computing.

Since I started graduate school, the Internet has become accessible, and email has become part of my work life. I used to use the blackboard and overhead projectors when teaching. Now, PowerPoint slides are ubiquitous. Not all the changes have been good. Some days, it takes me hours to get through my email. It is hard to imagine life before cell phones, but no doubt cell phones can be a distraction, leading to traffic accidents.

This chapter is about new things, how they catch on (or not), and the impacts the new things have. In Chapter 2, Professor David Berlo was introduced. He started some new things like departments of communication at American universities. As the founding department chair at Michigan State, he hired Gerald Miller (Chapter 4) and Everett Rogers (this chapter). Rogers is famous for the topic of this chapter, diffusion of innovations. I met Dr. Rogers only once at a communication conference. He had moved from Michigan State to the University of Southern California before I arrived at MSU. He finished his career at the University of New Mexico, and that was where he was teaching when I finally met him. But his book, *Diffusion of Innovations*, was the first book I read from cover to cover in graduate school. It was assigned the first week of class due by the start of the second week. The professor who assigned it (Dr. Virginia Richmond) said it was a must-read for communication students. At the time, I had never read anything like it. My appreciation for it has only grown over time. It certainly influenced the approach I took in my other book, *Duped*. Here, I will give you a summary of Roger's classic book.

In all, there have been five editions of Roger's *Diffusion of Innovations*. It is among the most influential books in academic communication and one of the most cited in all the social sciences. Last I checked, it had more than 100,000 citations on Google Scholar. This chapter, as I mentioned previously, is derived from, and based on, the various editions of Rogers's now classic work.[1]

Defining Diffusion of Innovations

An **innovation** is *something that is perceived as new*. It is any new thing. It can be an idea, practice, or a thing. **Diffusion** is how a new thing *spreads* among *adopters*. If the new thing catches on, it diffuses. These days, when

---

1. Rogers (2003).

something diffuses rapidly, we say it *goes viral*. Of course, some new things never catch on and don't diffuse. They "die on the vine," so to speak. Diffusion is a *process* that occurs over time, and it requires *communication* through *channels* and *networks* (see Chapter 21). Thus, *diffusion of innovations* is about how ideas spread (or not) among people or groups over time. Everything we know or use was an innovation at some point in the past. There was a time before electricity or flush toilets.

We can think of this book as an example of an innovation. It is a new sort of textbook, different from other books on human communication. The topics covered, the organizational structure of the book, and the narrative style reflect our new approach to this book. As I write this sentence, I don't know if the book will diffuse beyond UAB, where Dr. Shebib and I now teach. But it could. It might be picked up at other universities around the country or maybe even around the world. What will determine if it is adapted elsewhere? If it does diffuse, what determines how widely and how fast it spreads? What are the consequences, if any, of it being used elsewhere? Would this be a good thing, a bad thing, or a mixed bag? These are the sorts of questions raised when we think about diffusion of innovations. Time will tell if this book diffuses. Fortunately for us, there has been plenty of research on other innovations. While we cannot know how a particular innovation will play out, much is known about how the process works.

Parts of the Diffusions Process

According to Rogers, there are four main elements of the diffusion process. The first and most obvious is the innovation itself. The second is the **communication channels**. People can learn about innovations from friends face-to-face, from salespeople, from advertising, from social media, and the like. The third issue is *time*. How fast an innovation spreads is called the **rate of adoption**. Finally, the fourth issue is the *social system*. How interconnected are the people? Are people open to innovation and change? Is the innovation culturally appropriate? All innovations exist in larger social, cultural, historical, and political contexts.

Perceived Attributes of Innovations

One of the most important parts of the diffusion process is the nature of innovation itself and how people perceive the innovation. Rogers identified five aspects of innovations that matter for diffusion. These include relative advantage, compatibility, complexity, trialability, and observability. Think of *relative advantage* as perceived value-added. Is the innovation an improvement? How so, and how much? Is it worth the cost and effort to change? Regarding this book as an innovation, will people see it as better than other books on the market? Of course, the more relative advantage, the more likely an innovation is to be adopted.

The second consideration is *compatibility*. Most innovations need to work with other things to be successful. For example, a new smartphone app might be useful, but if it does not work on either Android or iPhone, it is unlikely to become popular. Innovations also need to be culturally compatible.

Generally speaking, *complexity* works against diffusion. The harder something is to understand, to use, or to implement, the less likely people are to try it. This is important because *trailability* enhances the chances of diffusion. If you can try something out first, it is seen as less risky, and you can see how you like it. The more complex it is, the less likely it is to make a good first impression. Even if an innovation cannot be tried first, if people can see it being used successfully by others (*observability*), it is more likely to diffuse.

Rogers grew up on a family farm in Iowa. Some agricultural scientists at Iowa State University created a new

CHAPTER 13

hybrid corn seed in 1928. The new seed (the innovation) had some clear relative advantages. It produced crops with higher yields that were better suited to mechanical harvesting and that were more drought resistant. The seed was compatible with their farming practices and no more complex than the old seeds. Farmers could buy it and plant it the same way as ever. Farmers could try it out on small plots first. They could also observe the crops on neighboring farms. The new seed had all the desirable perceived attributes of innovations. Over 13 years, 99% of the farmers adopted the new seed.

The Diffusion Curve

If an innovation spreads, we can plot its progress in a *diffusion curve*. In the curve, time is on the horizontal axis of the graph and the proportion of people who have adopted is on the vertical axis. Most innovations start off slowly. After progressing slowly, they may hit a *tipping point* where the *rate of adoption* increases at a faster rate. Once an innovation hits the tipping point, it is said to have *critical mass*. Then, eventually, the rate slows down again.

For example, with the Iowa corn seed, in the first 5 years, only 10% of the farmers adopted the new seed. Then it caught on, and 40% adopted over the next 5 years. Then the rate gradually leveled off until everyone who was going to adopt the seed was using it.

Cell phones showed a similar pattern. In the first decade, 130 million were sold. In the next decade, the number was 1.1 billion. Now, the rate of new adoption is slow because almost everyone has already started using a cell phone.

The Innovation Decision Process

Before an innovation comes about, there are important preexisting conditions. There are *prior practices, perceived needs*, the *openness* of people to new things, and the *norms* of the social system. Once the innovation is developed, the first step of the process is the *knowledge phase*. For diffusion to happen, potential adopters need to learn about the innovation. The second step is *persuasion*. Here, the perceived attributes of the innovation come into play. The more the innovation provides relative advantage, compatibility, less complexity, trialability, and observability, the more likely it is to be adopted in the decision phase. In the *decision phase*, people either adapt or reject the innovation. Next is the *implementation phase*. Adopters start using the innovation. The final phase is *confirmation*. Adopters can continue the adoption or discontinue adoption. People who earlier rejected the innovation can later decide to adopt or continue their rejection.

Diffusion Networks

Networks consist of interconnected people. Later, we will have a full chapter on networks. For now, both knowledge about innovations and influence regarding the desirability of innovations flow through communication networks. Some people within networks are more influential than others. **Opinion leaders** are people who are well-connected and influential. Successful innovations are usually pushed by opinion leaders. We could also call them *influencers*.

My major professor, Frank Boster, has researched what he calls **super diffusers**. These are the best opinion leaders. Super diffusers are high in connectedness, very persuasive, and are seen as *mavens*. Mavens are people who others see as knowledgeable.

Consequences of Innovations

Innovations change people's lives. Sometimes the change is small or incremental. Other innovations can be game changers. At the beginning of the chapter, I talked about going from a typewriter to a PC. For me and many others, that was big. Going from a monochrome monitor to VGA, to HD, to full HD, to a 4K display over the past 30 years has been an improvement but less life-changing.

The consequences of innovations can be good, bad, or very often a mix of good and bad. Consider fossil fuels. They made the industrial age possible. Transportation went from walking or riding horses to trains to cars to airplanes. We have gas stoves and the electrical grid. Few of us would want to go back to a time before fossil fuels. But there was the major downside of global warming. It turns out that all that carbon in the atmosphere is warming the planet and thereby changing climate and weather patterns in undesirable ways.

The consequences of innovations can also be anticipated or unanticipated. I doubt the inventors of the internal combustion engine foresaw the climate consequences. No one fully realized how the Internet or cell phones would change our lives.

Finally, the consequences of innovations can be direct or indirect. For example, the internal combustion engine led to the development of the automobile. As the people driving automobiles reached critical mass, the need for highways and gas stations emerged. Car companies built factories, and autoworkers formed unions, and so forth.

Chapter Summary

- An innovation is something that is perceived as new.
- Diffusion of innovations is the process of an innovation spreading and catching on.
- Not all innovations diffuse. Some fail to catch on.
- Innovations that offer relative advantage, compatibility, less complexity, trialability, and observability are more likely to diffuse.
- The diffusion curve reflects the rate of adoption over time.
- The consequences of innovations can be good or bad, anticipated or unanticipated, and direct or indirect.

Next, we turn to Dr. Shebib's discussion of nonverbal communication.

Unit III

Being Better Communicators

CHAPTER 14

Nonverbal Communication

[Dr. Shebib's Voice]

L et me take you back in time to where my love for nonverbal communication originated. I enrolled in a nonverbal communication class as an undergraduate student at ASU, but to be honest, I was just taking it because Dr. Laura Guerrero was the professor. At the time, I was already set on wanting to continue my education and pursue graduate degrees. I also knew that I needed recommendation letters from highly respected faculty and scholars. I just enrolled in the class to get on her good side and hopefully become a research assistant for her so she'd write me a recommendation letter for graduate school (spoiler, it all worked out that way, and she's literally amazing). Ironically, last month, I wrote *her* a recommendation letter for a huge teaching award from the International Association for Relationship Research. But the class, nonverbal communication, changed my life. **It literally changed my entire perspective on everything**.

As I have been writing this chapter, *Netflix* released a limited series called *Inventing Anna*. This limited series is based on a true story of Anna Sorokin/Delvey (except the parts that are totally made up—hence the irony). The *New York Times* reported that she stole a private jet and bilked banks, hotels, and associates out of about $200,000. She did all of this while attempting to secure a $25 million loan from a hedge fund to create an exclusive arts club. Swindling her way into a life of luxury, Anna deceived Manhattan's elite into believing she was a German heiress worth 60 million euros. Without spoiling the ending for those of you who are currently watching it or want to watch it, obviously, the deception and secrecy are inherent in the series. However, what stood out the most to me was nonverbal communication. You know, the whole "fake it till you make it" philosophy.

Julia Garner (Ruth from *Ozark*) plays Anna in the series. Garner's voice is a pitch-perfect imitation of Delvey's actual one, and her performance is another opportunity to show how the voice can articulate a strident range of emotions capable of summoning forth. The consistency of her self-assured body language and smug facial expressions communicates the character's self-certainty and sense of superiority. Is Anna Delvey despicable and vain? Absolutely. But Garner projects a kind of dense armor that makes her brief moments of vulnerability at least somewhat affecting. The problem is that the *who* of Anna Delvey is so slippery and inconsistent that any attempt to understand her seems fraught, and yet *Inventing Anna* spends hours rewinding, fast-forwarding, and ultimately tripping over itself trying to convince us (or even themselves) that the truth is malleable and subjective and in the eye of the beholder.

Throughout this chapter, I will illustrate and emphasize the power nonverbal communication plays in our daily interactions. Chapter 25 will focus on deception.

Defining Nonverbal Communication

Nonverbal communication refers to all aspects of communication that do not involve the spoken word or written language. Instead, it refers to nonword behaviors and "how" behaviors, such as body language, facial expressions, eye behavior, and use of space to communicate messages. Think of the phrase, "It's not what you say, but how you say it." This also refers to nonverbal communication, and more specifically, vocalics, which I'll discuss more in a bit. Much of the emotional meaning of messages comes from nonverbal communication.

Functions of Nonverbal Communication

Nonverbal communication plays five key functions in the communication process.[1] First, nonverbal communication can *reinforce* the verbal message. This can help make messages clearer and help avoid potential misunderstandings that might arise. Second, nonverbal communication can *substitute* for the verbal message (e.g., shaking hands or waving goodbye instead of saying "hello" or "goodbye"). Third, nonverbal communication can *contradict* verbal messages. A classic example is sarcasm. Sarcastic people are good at saying the opposite of what they think by contradicting words and adding vocalic indicators. Fourth, nonverbal communication can *accentuate* the verbal message. By accentuate, I mean putting emphasis on something said. And finally, fifth, nonverbal communication can *regulate* the flow of conversations. For example, raising your hand in class indicates to me you have something to say. I call on you and turn the conversation over to you so you can ask your question or make a comment.

Nonverbal communication is versatile and an extremely influential tool. You must be competent in nonverbal communication to be a competent communicator. Words alone will not get you there. Mastery can help you become a better speaker, persuader, worker, and partner. It can help you lead good and meaningful conversations. It can also help you express your intentions and deliver your messages better. Remember that it can cause misunderstandings too. People give different meanings to nonverbal cues. So, it's a good tip to know your audience before you speak. Be clear on your intentions and work hard to be a better communicator. Remember also that words and nonverbal behaviors work in tandem and need to be in sync with each other.

Nonverbal Codes

To understand nonverbal communication, we need to understand what a code is first. Codes were brought up back in Chapter 2, where Berlo's SMCR provided a code model of communication. A *code* is a set of signals that is usually transmitted via one particular medium or channel (such as the voice or the body). Codes are organized message systems consisting of a set of symbols and rules for their use. Nonverbal communication consists of a variety of different codes. Researchers[2] classify the various nonverbal behaviors into different categories of nonverbal codes. These nonverbal codes consist of kinesics, oculesics, proxemics, haptics, chronemics, vocalics, physical appearance, and artifacts. These are all different aspects of nonverbal communication, and within these, there are subtypes.

1. Ekman and Friesen (1969).
2. Burgoon et al. (2010).

Kinesics

Kinesics refers to messages sent from the body. They include facial expressions, emblems, gestures, posture, body movement, body lean, and so forth. Kinesics is one of the most influential nonverbal codes because of its visibility and the wealth of features available for influencing messages.

Of all possible facial expressions, smiling has probably been studied the most. Research has shown that by smiling, waitresses earn more tips,[3] therapists are judged to be warmer and more competent, job interviewees create positive impressions of themselves and are more likely to get jobs, female hitchhikers get more rides, students accused of cheating are treated with greater leniency, and teachers inspire students to pay more attention when smiling.[4] In general, smiling facilitates persuasion because it conveys warmth and immediacy. However, there are some exceptions. First, fleeting smiles, which occur quickly, can be an exception. One study found that when smiles appear quickly, the smiling person is perceived as less trustworthy and attractive than when smiles have a slower onset.[5] Second, disingenuous smiles are perceived as less persuasive than genuine ones. Third, smiling may not fit the situation. For example, there are situations where a smile isn't socially appropriate.

According to communication accommodation theory, rather than using any one type of nonverbal behavior, a persuader should try to build rapport with others by mirroring or mimicking their nonverbal cues.[6] In other words, smile when people smile and frown when people frown. Facial expressions that make a person seem sociable and relaxed and that "mirror" the audience's expressions tend to increase the influence seeker's persuasiveness. One interesting thing about facial expression is that researchers have found that if you make the facial expression, you also begin feeling the emotion yourself! Emotions not only cause facial expressions—facial expressions also help you feel emotions. This is referred to as the facial feedback hypothesis.[7]

Emblems are kinesic nonverbal behaviors that substitute words but have precise verbal meaning. Some common examples of emblems in the United States are the "OK" gesture and the "shush" gesture. Using emblems appropriately within a culture is of utmost importance. For example, former president Richard Nixon when president, he visited Venezuela and was giving a speech and gave two "OK" sign gestures to the crowd. Suddenly, a huge riot erupted. He didn't know this—but the "OK" gesture has a different meaning in Venezuela, like that of an upraised middle finger in America! Whoops! Emblems provide more visual information to the message, which may help audience members' attention and retention of the message.

Illustrators accompany speech by emphasizing what is being said. Illustrators depend on but also add an emphasis to, verbal messages. For example, pointing my finger to emphasize a point or slamming my fist on the desk to articulate my point are examples of illustrators. None of these gestures has a meaning in and of itself, as an emblem would.

Although illustrators seem to increase people's persuasiveness, *adaptors* tend to decrease persuasiveness. There are two forms of adaptors: self-adaptors and object adaptors. *Self-adaptors* are manipulations of your own body. For example, twisting or brushing your hand through your hair. *Object adaptors*, on the other hand, are material objects used in the tension management process. For example, tapping a pencil on your desk, chewing on a straw, or playing with your necklace. The only communicative value seems to be that they tell people we

---

3. Tidd and Lockard (1978).
4. Saigh (1981).
5. Krumhuber et al. (2007).
6. Giles and Wiemann (1987).
7. Ekman et al. (1983).

might be nervous or uncomfortable. "Might be" is key here because they might just be a habit or mean nothing at all. People, nevertheless, tend to see them as communicating nervousness and anxiety. Adapts, of course, can signal that. The main point to remember is that adaptors inhibit persuasion and should be avoided if possible. They create impressions of a lack of composure and nervousness, which reduces trustworthiness.

Oculesics

Oculesics refers to the study of eye behavior. In general, eye contact facilitates persuasion. Maintaining eye contact can (a) increase perceptions of intelligence, (b) increase compliance with requests, (c) increase perceived credibility, (d) reduce perceptions of exclusion, and (e) reduce defensiveness.

A classic study[8] illustrates that the effectiveness of eye contact may depend on other factors, such as the legitimacy of the request you make. In the study, persuaders were instructed to approach people in an airport and ask them for money. Some of the targets were told that the money would be used to make an important phone call (a legitimate request), whereas others were told that the money would be used to pay for a candy bar or gum (an illegitimate request). It turned out that people who thought the persuader needed to make a phone call gave more money, but only when the persuader looked at them. Interestingly, however, eye contact decreased compliance when the persuader made an illegitimate request. Perhaps, as the researcher suggested, looking away while making an illegitimate request makes a person seem more humble or embarrassed, thereby increasing his or her persuasiveness by winning the sympathy of others.

Haptics

Haptics refers to the use of touch. Touch is important for emotional and psychological well-being, starting from the time we spend in the womb and extending into old age.[9] A series of famous studies by Harlow and his colleagues[10] helps illustrate the importance of touch. In these studies, infant monkeys were raised in isolation from their mothers. The experimenters then set up two types of "surrogate mothers": a hard wire mesh "mother" that supplied food through a bottle and a soft terrycloth-covered "mother" equipped with a light bulb for warmth. The infant monkeys spent up to 18 hours a day clinging to the warm terrycloth-covered mothers. In contrast, they visited the wire mothers only long enough to get nourishment. Harlow and his colleagues concluded that contact comfort was a primary need in higher order mammals. The infant monkeys in these studies were clearly more attached to the mothers who provided them with warmth and touch than to those who provided them with food. Therefore, although food is essential for survival, touch is more important when it comes to providing emotional security.

In relation to persuasion, touch facilitates compliance gaining. However, it must be appropriate in nature and light. The persuasive impact of touch has been demonstrated in other contexts as well. For example, light touch has been found to increase the number of people who volunteer,[11] sign petitions,[12] complete

---

8. Kleinke (1980).

9. Reite (1990).

10. Harlow (1958), Harlow et al. (1963), and Harlow and Zimmerman (1958).

11. Patterson et al. (1986).

12. Willis and Hamm (1980).

questionnaires,[13] and more. Similarly, when food servers touch diners appropriately, the servers earn higher tips,[14] and the diners are more likely to take the servers' recommendations about what to order.[15] Overall, a light and appropriate touch facilitates sales of a product.

Proxemics

Proxemics refers to the perception, use, and structuring of space as communication. When there is space between people, the amount of space and the degree to which space is connected to one's territory have implications for the interaction at hand. Just as people need touch to feel close and connected, so too do people need space to maintain privacy and personal space. Conversational distances are most notable when discussing proxemics and communication. There are four perceptual categories of conversational distance: intimate, personal-casual, social-consultative, and public.[16] These categories refer to the amount of space that a communicator places between her or himself and others. Note that these conversational distance zones were created based on observations in North America and may not apply in other cultures.

The *intimate distance* range stretches from 0 to 1½ feet, meaning that people are literally at or within arm's reach when communicating at this distance. In the intimate zone, sensory stimulation is particularly high. Clearly, intimate distance is typically reserved for private, informal interaction with people we like and trust.

The *personal-casual distance* ranges from 1½ to 4 feet. This is divided into two categories. First, the personal distance ranges from 1½ to 2½ feet, while the casual distance is the rest, 2½ to 4 feet. Personal conversation is likely to take place at both of these distances; however, the content of conversation is likely to be somewhat less intimate at the casual distance than the personal distance.

The *social-consultative distance* ranges from 4 to 10 feet. This is again split into two categories. The first, social, ranges from 4 to 7 feet, where more impersonal social conversations are engaged. The social zone provides people with sufficient space to maintain some level of privacy in that others are not close enough to touch or smell them. Second is the consultative, which ranges from 7 to 10 feet. Here, more formal interaction, such as business transactions, takes place. In both the social and consultative, communicators have easier access to multiple communication channels (e.g., they are less restricted to looking at the face), and they can more easily avert their attention from the conversation at hand. They do not, however, have access to minute facial expressions.

Finally, *public distance* ranges from 10 feet onward. Public distance typically occurs in formal settings, such as between speakers and their audiences, celebrities who are blocked off from their fans, or powerful CEOs meeting with groups of lower-level employees. In these situations, communication often involves many people focusing on a single communicator. The audience has an overall view of the person rather than being able to focus on the communicator's facial expressions or eye behavior.

Chronemics

Less research has paid attention to **chronemics**, or the study of how time is used to communicate. Time can be an

13. Vaidis and Halimi-Falkowicz (2008).
14. Hornick (1992).
15. Guéguen et al. (2007).
16. Hall (1959, 1990).

important commodity, especially in a culture like the United States. Thus, not showing up on time and being late can have implications for the way others might perceive you. For example, research found that people who arrive 15 minutes late are considered dynamic but much less competent, composed, and sociable than people who arrive on time.[17]

However, we know speaking time is related to dominance, especially for men. Powerful people are allowed to speak longer and have more speaking turns, which gives them more opportunities to influence others. Waiting time also reflects power; waiting is the fate of the powerless, as people are generally waiting for the powerful. Medical doctors are notorious for doing this; we wait so long sometimes during doctor visits. Essentially, the higher your status, the more power you have over other people's time. Time not only affects the perceptions of people but also can be used as a persuasive tactic and ploy. For example, by providing people with limited time to purchase a product, they may be more persuaded to buy it—this is referred to as scarcity. People want more of those things they can have less of.

Vocalics

Vocalics refer to how you say the words rather than what you are actually saying. It includes changes in speaking rate, volume, voice quality, pitch, accents, pauses, and hesitations. It also includes silence and accents. Use the following QR code to see Garner's accent for Anna on my TikTok account. Vocalics can change the meaning of words. According to the "what sounds beautiful is good" hypothesis, voices that are rated as more attractive are associated with better qualities and are also rated as more persuasive.[18] In one study,[19] for instance, people who listened to high-pitched voices perceived the speaker as more attractive and extroverted than those who listened to low-pitched voices. Similarly, researchers[20] found that when managers spoke clearly and varied their tone, employees tended to like them better.

More recently, researchers have identified a quality of voice known as vocal fry or "creaky voice," which is characterized by drawing out the end of sentences with a low, croaking growl in the back of the throat. It is perceived as less competent, less trustworthy, less attractive, and less hirable. In addition to pitch and quality, researchers have examined the effects of speaking rate. Previous studies, for example, indicate that faster speakers, to an extent, are perceived as more credible[21] and persuasive[22] compared to those who speak slower,

17. Burgoon et al. (1996).
18. Zuckerman and Driver (1989).
19. Imhof (2010).
20. Hinkle (2001).
21. Simonds et al. (2006).
22. Miller et al. (1976).

perhaps because they appear more competent and knowledgeable. This, too, however, may not apply in other cultures, such as Asia, where slower speech may be considered more thoughtful and wiser.

Additionally, researchers[23] found that for persuasion to occur, the optimal rate of speech may depend on both the encoding ability of the sender and the decoding ability of the receiver. Specifically, although good decoders were more likely to comply with speeches delivered at fast rates, poor decoders preferred slower rates.

There has also been a lot of research on effective pauses and silence to make points and arguments. Used appropriately and effectively, they can lead to persuasion as well. You might be interested to know that not all studies on vocalics focus exclusively on human speech.

Indeed, for those of you who've been unfortunate enough to answer your telephone and find one of those eerie computer-synthesized voices selling some product on the other end, here's an interesting study.[24] The study asked people to listen to persuasive messages spoken by either a natural human voice or a synthetic computerized voice and then measured how persuaded the people were. Surprisingly, the results indicated that the synthetic voice was just as persuasive as the human voice.

Physical Appearance

Attractive people are judged to be happier, more intelligent, friendlier, stronger, and kinder and are thought to have better personalities, better jobs, and greater marital competence.[25] Generally, physically attractive people are more persuasive. The halo effect attempts to explain this, essentially the hypothesis deemed "what is beautiful is good."[26] In other words, if the person is attractive, he or she must also be trustworthy, well-informed, and so forth. However, the halo effect isn't limited to the way we look at people. It can also affect the way that we judge other things, such as products and companies. This means, for example, that if you have a positive impression of a certain brand, you are more likely to buy products from that brand, even if the positive impression that you have of them is not directly related to the product at hand.

Businesses can use the halo effect as a persuasive strategy. In business and as a persuasion strategy, we consistently see this strategy employed in a few ways: (a) celebrity endorsements (or appeal to authority), (b) the use of beautiful people, (c) beautiful design (or making a good first impression), (d) corporate (big) names, and (e) using different language like "organic." One study that particularly looked at the halo effect found that the word "organic" on products was associated with more likely to purchase and willingness to pay more money for it.

Artifacts

The clothes and makeup we wear, the cars we drive, the furniture we own, and other physical objects, also known as *artifacts*, can communicate a great deal about our credibility and status. In our society, material goods are viewed as an extension of oneself. As human beings, we make quick, snap judgments, whether right or wrong, about people based on physical appearance and artifacts.

23. Buller and Aune (1988).
24. Stern et al. (1999).
25. Knapp (1992).
26. Dion et al. (1972).

Previous literature suggests that first impressions are not only powerful and enduring, but they are also often based on seemingly trivial appearance cues. Research indicates, for example, that cues such as clothing, grooming, cosmetics, hair length, tattooing, and body piercing influence judgments about credibility, attractiveness, and whether to hire someone. In other words, if anything, such research indicates that such cues are not trivial at all and, in some contexts (e.g., when interviewing), may be more important than verbal cues.

Artifacts and features of the environment can be influential. For instance, power and status might be communicated through the size and location of a person's office. Large offices in corner spaces, for example, are often considered prestigious.[27] Real estate agents manipulate the environment all the time. Right? They might "stage" the house by using decluttering and inexpensive improvements, which helps the house look bigger and cleaner to sell. Supermarkets are another example of how environments are arranged strategically. You might notice that staples such as dairy, meat, and produce are in the back or on opposite sides of the store. Why? It forces shoppers to meander through the aisles, where they'll be tempted to buy all kinds of other goodies. You'll also notice that chips, dips, and other products that "go together" are intentionally placed side by side, encouraging additional purchases.

Considerable evidence shows that artifacts and physical features of the environment can not only make products more noticeable, and people appear more (or less) credible, but they can also lead to persuasion. Most of this research has focused on the impact of clothing. Something about a uniform tends to make us obedient. We are more likely to comply with law enforcement and health-care officials when in uniform compared to when they are not. Fancy suits, uniforms, and high-status clothing are related to higher rates of compliance.[28] In some cases, it may also be possible to influence people by wearing clothing that makes them identify with a persuader. Research,[29] for instance, found that well-dressed people were more persuasive in airports, but casually dressed people were more persuasive at bus stops. It appears that artifacts, particularly clothing, make a difference when trying to seek compliance. Of course, artifacts can also affect your appearance or attractiveness, which, in turn, can affect your persuasiveness.

Chapter Summary

- The various nonverbal codes affect message content.
- Kinesics refers to body movement, gestures, emblems, and facial expressions.
- Oculesics refers to eye behavior.
- Proxemics refers to the use of space.
- Haptics refers to the use of touch.
- Chronemics refers to the use of time.
- Vocalics refer to the way in which words are spoken.
- Physical attractiveness and artifacts are also nonverbal codes that influence communicative interactions, especially first impressions.

27. Andersen (1999).
28. Segrin (1993).
29. Hensley (1981).

As you can tell, I could keep going on about nonverbal communication, but you could always just take the nonverbal communication course with me! Additionally, check out nonverbal TikToks on my @ShebibSquad TikTok channel. In the next chapter, Dr. Levine will discuss culture and communication.

CHAPTER 15

Culture and Communication

[Dr. Levine's Voice]

I left MSU in 2013 to take a faculty position at Korea University in Seoul. I lived as a foreigner for 2 years in a country where I did not speak the language. Fortunately, I taught classes in English. Students at Korea University are required to take some classes in English, and almost all Korean professors (understandably) would rather teach in Korean. I taught human communication (among other classes) in English there.

It was a good experience. I am happy I did it. I came away from my adventure with a perspective that I would not have otherwise. I learned what it was like being a foreigner and minority (albeit a high-status one), and I experienced a different culture. There were also many things I liked about living there. My Internet was faster, and my cell coverage was better. I did not have a car and used public transportation, which worked well. I was shocked at the affordability of health care. Things are convenient and work well in Seoul.

There were some things I didn't like. The air quality was often poor; there was too much air pollution. The weather is not the best. It is too cold in winter and too hot in summer. I can also do without the 12-hour flights and 13-hour time changes involved visiting the United States for a conference or to see family.

My big takeaway from living and working in Korea is that I am now more skeptical of sweeping generalities regarding cultural differences. Don't get me wrong. Culture is important. It affects communication, and cultural differences exist. This said, I have three "buts" to add. First up, it is my experience that many cultural differences belie deeper similarities in human behavior. For example, the rules for how to be polite are different. Do I bow, shake hands, or both? It is, however, important to be polite everywhere. People are doing the same thing, just enacting it differently. That is, there are different rules, but the underlying functions are the same.

Second, you just cannot presume that because a person is from a culture, they are a certain way. Everyone is different, and competent communication involves not just cultural literacy but appreciating individual variation within cultures. There is a natural tendency when we meet a person from a culture that is new to us to presume that our observations of the person's actions tell us something about their culture and vice versa. Often, it is just them. There is as much person-to-person variability in Koreans as Americans. I met some nice people and some real jerks. Some Korean students were talkative in class; others were quiet.

Third, many generalizations I had read about cultures were either wrong or overapplied. I have read that Asians are not direct in communication, but I have witnessed communication among Asians that is extremely direct, even by American standards. There are contexts where Koreans are more likely to be direct than Americans, such as a professor giving a student feedback about a poorly done assignment. In some ways, Koreans are collectivistic, but there are also ways that Koreans are individualistic, just as there are ways in which Americans are collective.

Four Considerations

My current thinking is that human social behavior is a function of four types of influences. Down deep, there are things common to all humans that come with being human. There is also person-to-person variation or individual differences. Everyone is different, and each of us has our own unique version of being human that is idiosyncratic to us. There are also situational and contextual influences on peoples' behaviors. It matters whether people are at home, at work, at school, or out with friends. Culture lies on top of deep human-nature communality and individual differences. It makes people who are from the same social groups have things in common that are not shared by people from different cultures, and it provides rules for how to act in different situations.

Earlier, I used the example of politeness. It is a general human rule that people need to be polite in their dealings with others. Humans everywhere are social, and we need communication and interaction rules to smooth social functioning. It is also a general rule that politeness is more important in formal situations and in interactions with people with whom we are less close.

This said some people are more inclined to be polite than others. Some people are blunt, relatively oblivious to others, or even rude. Others tend to be extremely concerned with etiquette and convention. Most people are somewhere in between the extremes. On top of this, cultures dictate how to enact politeness. People in one culture will follow different rules for being polite than people from a different culture. But all cultures have rules for politeness, and within all cultures, some people are more polite than others, and being polite is more important in some situations than others.

Defining Culture, Intercultural Communication, and Cross-Cultural Communication

The ideas most central to defining culture are that (a) it is *learned*, (b) it is *shared by groups* of people, (c) *different groups have different cultures*, and (d) it is *passed down* from generation to generation within groups. It is the shared attitudes, values, beliefs, conventions, and norms of a group that distinguishes the group from other groups. It includes language, religion, food, art, and music, among other learned social practices.

A useful definition is provided by Gerd Hofstede, who, closely paraphrasing, defines culture as *the collective programming of the mind that distinguishes the members of one group of people from another.*[1] Hofstede is among the most influential figures in cross-cultural communication. The programming aspect suggests that culture is learned and that humans are born ready to learn and absorb culture. His use of the word "collective" means that culture is shared with a group, but each group will have its own version of culture.

Intercultural communication is the interaction between people from different cultures. **Cross-cultural communication** involves making comparisons between cultures. For example, when I was living in Korea, I was engaging in intercultural communication every time I interacted with a Korean. If I mention a general difference between Korean culture and American culture, then that is a cross-cultural difference. Cross-cultural communication involves systematic differences between cultures. These differences are often understood as varying along several dimensions.

---

1. Hofstede (2001).

Cultural Dimensions

Dimensions, as often used in the social sciences, refer to continua (the plural of continuum) along which things vary. For example, we can think of social anxiety as a continuum ranging from maximally anxious to not at all anxious. Any given person at any given time will occupy a spot along the social anxiety continuum, and different people can be thought of as more or less prone to social anxiety. Just as the anxiety dimension is one way to understand a person's personality and how people differ in personality, cultural dimensions are ways that cultures differ.

For our discussion here, three cultural dimensions are highlighted: individualism-collectivism, high-low power-distance, and high-low context communication. The first two come from Hofstede, and the third from Edward T. Hall.

Individualism-collectivism is the most well-known and influential cultural dimension. As the name implies, *individualistic cultures* focus on people as individuals and their individuality (excuse the circularity). People are expected to be themselves. Autonomy, freedom, and uniqueness are valued. North America, the United Kingdom, Western Europe, Australia, and New Zealand are usually considered examples of individualistic cultures.

Collectivist cultures, in contrast, see people as belonging to *in-groups*. Conformity is prioritized. Competition in collectivistic societies is between groups rather than between individuals. Many Asian and African cultures are high on collectivism, especially China.[2]

Cultural individualism-collectivism is thought to influence how people understand themselves. When applied to people's self-concepts, these go by *independent and interdependent self-construal*.[3] Independent self-construal reflects individualism, while interdependent self-construal reflects collectivism. A person with an independent self-construal understands themselves as a unique person with characteristics that differentiate them from others. Those with interdependent self-construals understand themselves as members of relationships and groups.

The second main cultural dimension is *power distance*. This refers to the importance of hierarchy in a culture. High power-distance cultures are more top-down. Higher status people are respected and obeyed, and everyone is expected to accept power differences as legitimate. Low power-distance cultures are more egalitarian. No one should have too much power; power is more distributed, and people are even sometimes skeptical of those in power. Russia, China, India, and countries in the Middle East are high power distance, while Australia, New Zealand, and the Scandinavian countries are the lowest in power distance.

Korea, for example, is higher in power distance than the United States. This is one of the first things I noticed teaching in Korea. The distance between students and teachers is greater. Students are more respectful and use honorifics when addressing professors. I wasn't just Professor Levine; I was Professor Levine-Nim (-nim is an honorific). When I walked into a building or room, students would sometimes bow. Students might get professors' drinks, such as coffee for class. As a professor in Korea, I could certainly ask a student to get me a coffee, although I didn't do that. While America has lower power difference than Korea, there are regional differences. UAB students typically call me Dr. Levine, whereas students at MSU would often use my first name. There are also institutional differences in power distance. For example, both UAB and MSU are more hierarchical, where subordinates do not question those above them on the organizational chart. The University of Hawaii,

2. Oyserman et al. (2002).
3. Markus and Kitayama (1991).

in contrast, had strong faculty governance, and consequently, faculty had much more say in university decision-making.

The final dimension is *high-low context communication*. You may have heard the expression that some quote was *taken out of context*. That expression means that the quote is misunderstood and means something different if it is understood in the situation it came from or along with preceding or subsequent parts of the statement. The idea is that some verbal statements need additional knowledge or background to understand. Other statements are perfectly understandable standing alone—all you need to know is the language and what the words mean. Statements that can stand alone and still be understood are low context. High-context communication requires additional knowledge to understand. For example, if I say, "I am writing a draft chapter of a book right now," you have the context to know that I am working on this book. However, if you overheard me saying that on the phone to someone, you would not know which book I was working on unless you knew I was working on this one. If I am talking with my friend Steve about someone being "Kimmed," you might guess that some named Kim was being referenced in a less than flattering way, but you would need to know the back story to know the reference. Similarly, if you did not follow American Politics, you might not get many of the jokes on the *Daily Show* or the cold openings to *Saturday Night Live*. Satire is high context. You must know what is being satirized.

High-low context communication is often considered a cultural dimension. Communication in Asian cultures, especially Japan, is seen as subtle and indirect, requiring cultural understanding beyond just knowing the language. Communication in America, in contrast, is presented as direct, straightforward, and low context.

I have a different take on high-low context communication. I see it as an intercultural dimension more than a cross-cultural dimension. Much communication is high context to the cultural outsider. I have no doubt that most Americans trying to get by in an Asian country see communication as high context. I suspect that international students in America also see Americans' communication as high context. This is not just about differences in nation-cultures. If you are talking to a group of people who are all friends with each other, but you are not in their circle, their communication with each other will be high context to you.

Chapter Summary

- Culture is learned, it is shared by groups of people, different groups have different cultures, and culture is passed down from generation to generation within groups.
- Intercultural communication involves interaction between people from different cultures, whereas cross-cultural communication involves making comparisons between cultures.
- Individualism-collectivism, power-distance, and high-low context communication are dimensions used to compare cultures.
- Although that culture influences how we communicate, not all members of a culture are the same or act in a particular way.

Next up, Dr. Shebib will talk about sex differences and similarities in communication and discuss the role of gender in human communication.

_____

CHAPTER 16

Sex, Gender, and Beyond the Binary

[*Dr. Shebib's Voice*]

In my first semester at UAB, during the fall of 2021, Dr. Levine and I team taught our introduction to human communication course. First off, I was extremely nervous to team teach for an entire semester with the chair of my new department during my first semester as an assistant professor. However, we worked seamlessly together. We both offered unique perspectives regarding communication phenomena, which provided a more nuanced view of human behavior. While Dr. Levine and I have commonalities, for example, both starting off as psychology majors before switching to communication, and we both received our doctorates in communication from MSU, we also have several differences (e.g., sex and age/generational differences).

After teaching the course, during the spring semester, I was approached by a student who took the course both Dr. Levine and I team taught. They said to me, "I thought you were just a TA." I was slightly shocked when I first heard them say that. But as the conversation progressed, I started to understand the attributions (see Chapter 18) that students might have made in the class. For example, I am younger than Dr. Levine. I am an early career professor who is probably closer in age to my students than I am to the more senior career professors in our department. Sex differences between male and female professors can manifest themselves in a variety of ways. Female professors often face unique challenges, including implicit bias, gender stereotypes, and a lack of representation. On the other hand, male professors may encounter expectations related to assertiveness and leadership.

When talking about sex and gender, it's important to ground this discussion with some basic definitions. **_Biological sex_** refers to an individual's biological makeup.[1] Sex differences, then, are typically about differences between groups of men and women. **_Gender_**, on the other hand, refers to how masculine, feminine, or androgynous a person is.[2] The effects of gender identity can be thought of as the combined impacts of masculinity and femininity across individuals (and within sexes). In essence, sex is biologically determined, whereas gender is socially, culturally, and psychologically constructed.

Sex Similarities and Differences in Communication

People often believe that men and women communicate differently. Common assumptions of sex differences, however, just aren't supported by research, which often finds more similarities than differences. All women are not the same; all men aren't the same either, and you just can't tell how someone will communicate based on whether they are male or female. Some of the research on sex differences is covered in this chapter.

1. Bem (1978).
2. Bem (1974).

In this chapter, sex similarities and differences are expressed in "effect size." These are units of "standard deviations." An effect size of 0 means that the average for men and the average for women are identical on something. That means there is no difference between men and women. An effect size of 1.0 would mean that they are about a standard deviation apart. Most effect sizes in social science are quite a bit smaller than that. An effect size of .2 or less is considered small, .4 or .5 is moderate, and .8 or bigger is large. But these are just rules of thumb.

What People Look for in a Partner?

What do people look for in a romantic partner? Do these differ between men and women? Well, researchers[3] examined this. They found 13 characteristics that people look for in a partner: (1) kind and understanding, (2) exciting personality, (3) intelligent, (4) physical attraction, (5) healthy, (6) easygoing, (7) creative, (8) wants children, (9), college graduate, (10) good earning capacity, (11) good heredity, (12) good housekeeper, and (13) religious. Out of these 13 characteristics that were identified, Buss and Barnes found only three to be significantly different between men and women: physical attractiveness, college graduates, and good earning capacity. Men rated physical attraction higher than women in terms of preferences regarding potential mates. Women, in contrast, rated being a college graduate and having a good earning capacity higher than men in terms of preferences regarding potential mates. The differences were not large.

Sexuality

Are there sex differences in sexuality? A meta-analysis[4] used 177 studies with over 125,000 participants. Results revealed some sex differences regarding sexuality. First, the researchers found that men have a more positive attitude about casual sex compared to women, with an effect size of .81, a large effect. Additionally, they found that men had slightly lower sexual satisfaction than women. This effect size was very small, at .06. Men reported a greater number of partners (.25) and reported having sex more often compared to women (with an effect size of .31).

Talkativeness

In a study,[5] 396 participants carried around a voice recorder for several days. The researchers developed a method for recording natural language using this electronic activated recorder (EAR). The EAR is a digital voice recorder that unobtrusively tracks people's real-world, moment-to-moment interactions. It operates by periodically recording snippets of ambient sounds, including conversations, while participants go about their daily lives. Because of the covert digital recording, it is impossible for participants to control or even to sense when the EAR is on or off.

For this study, the EAR was used to track naturally spoken words and to estimate how many words women and men use over the course of a day. They addressed the question about sex differences in daily word use with

3. Buss and Barnes (1986).
4. Oliver and Hyde (1993).
5. Mehl et al. (2007).

data from 6 samples based on 396 participants (210 women and 186 men) that were conducted between 1998 and 2004. Five of those samples were composed of university students within the United States, and the sixth were university students in Mexico. The data suggest that women spoke on average 16,215 words and men 15,669 words over an assumed period of, on average, 17 waking hours. Expressed in a common effect-size metric (Cohen's d = .07), this sex difference in daily word use (546 words) is tiny. Further, the difference does not meet conventional thresholds for statistical significance. Thus, the data fail to reveal a reliable sex difference in daily word use. Women and men both use, on average, about 16,000 words per day.

Smiling

In terms of smiling differences among men and women, a meta-analysis[6] was conducted. There was a total of 162 studies in the meta-analysis, with a total sample of greater than 100,000 participants. The researchers found that women do indeed smile more than men, and that effect size was represented in Cohen's d of .41, which is moderate. These results held up around the world, across various ethnicities, and over the life span.

These results are compatible with both a socialization explanation and an evolutionary one. In terms of the former, children are seen to gradually acquire an understanding of display rules through socialization processes that direct girls to show positive emotions and boys to hide vulnerable ones. Moreover, sex differences in emotion (or its expressions) may serve the adaptive purpose of helping men and women fulfill different societal roles. Socialization pressures may be particularly acute for adolescents and young adults as they move into sex-differentiated societal roles but diminish thereafter.

Evolutionary theorists view facial expressions as adaptive. According to this perspective, sex differences evolved early in human history as the result of males and females facing different selective pressures based on their reproductive strategies. Because of their assumed greater parental investment, women presumably acquired the tendency to smile more than men as a means of establishing secure bonds with their mate and their children via communication of positive emotion.

Risk-Taking

Risk-taking is "any consciously or nonconsciously controlled behavior with a perceived uncertainty about its outcome, and/or about its possible benefits or costs for the physical, economic or social well-being of oneself or others."[7] Researchers conducted a meta-analysis to see if sex differences exist within risk-taking behavior. The meta-analysis[8] consisted of 150 studies with a total sample of participants greater than 100,000.

The results found that male participants are more likely to take risks than female participants. In nearly every case, the mean effect size for a given type of risk (e.g., smoking, drinking, sexual activities) was significantly greater than 0, and almost half of the effect sizes were larger than .20, which is the conventional cutoff for small effects.

However, a more qualified interpretation of their results is that sex differences in risk-taking varied

6. LaFrance et al. (2003).

7. Trimpop (1994).

8. Brynes et al. (1999).

according to the context and age level. That is, sex differences in certain risky activities varied by age with age (e.g., driving), whereas others were associated with small sex differences regardless of age (e.g., smoking). Still others were associated with shifts from positive to negative effects as children grow older (e.g., sexual activities). Further still, most differences dropped off after age 21. The average effect size was just .13, which is small.

Aggression

A meta-analysis[9] of 107 studies of sex differences in aggression found that men are more aggressive, with an effect size of .24. They also found that people, in general, are more aggressive when they are provoked, with an effect size of .76. Their major goal was to assess whether provocation affects the magnitude of sex differences in aggression. As they expected, men were more aggressive than women under neutral conditions. The mean effect size was of moderate magnitude (.33). When provoked, men were more aggressive than women as well. However, the effect size was smaller (.17).

Interruptions

Next up, a meta-analysis[10] of 43 published studies was carried out to address the controversial issue of whether women or men are more likely to interrupt their conversational partners. First, a significant effect indicated that men were more likely than women to initiate interruptions. However, the corresponding effect size was small ($d =$ .15). Curiously, the first author's sex was a significant moderator. Studies report significantly larger effect sizes for men interrupting women when the lead author was female.

Specifically, women authors were more likely than men authors to report that men interrupted more than women. When effect sizes were analyzed, there was even a tendency for male authors to report the opposite finding; that is, male authors tended to report women interrupting more than men. The difference between women and men authors potentially reflects some form of researcher bias: some women researchers may be biased toward identifying men as more dominant than women, but it is also possible that male researchers may be biased toward identifying men as more dominant than women.

However, the researchers also note that there are substantial differences in how researchers operationalize (that is, measure) interruptions. Sometimes interruptions are measured as a form of domineering behavior that takes away the person's ability to talk with the intent of demonstrating dominance. Other times, interruptions are operationalized as including back-channel listening responses or affiliative overlaps that can demonstrate enthusiasm, agreement, or rapport. Therefore, any analysis of conversational interruptions should consider the multiple meanings of interruptions. Regardless of your sex and gender, it is best to avoid interrupting others.

Self-Disclosure

A meta-analysis[11] of 205 studies of sex differences in self-disclosure involving 23,702 subjects, published between

---

9. Bettencourt and Miller (1996).

10. Anderson and Leaper (1998).

11. Dindia and Allen (1992).

the years 1958 and 1989, was conducted. The results of the meta-analysis yielded a mean weighted effect size of d = .18. However, the effect size was not homogeneous across studies. Sex differences in self-disclosure were influenced by several moderator variables.

The first moderating variable was the sex of the target. Results revealed that females disclosed more than males to female and same-sex partners, slightly more than males to opposite-sex partners, but no more than males to male partners. In addition, sex differences in self-disclosure were significantly greater for female and same-sex targets than for opposite-sex and male targets.

Leadership

In terms of leadership, meta-analyses[12] have found small sex differences. First, let's consider the outcome of overall effectiveness. No sex differences emerged for overall leadership effectiveness. Additionally, when looking at the difference between people versus task focus, again, no sex differences emerged here. However, the researchers did find sex differences in terms of democratic versus autocratic leadership styles. Democratic leadership style refers to leaders who behave democratically and allow subordinates to participate in decision-making processes. Autocratic leadership style is when leaders behave autocratically and discourage subordinates from participating in decision-making. Results from this meta-analysis showed that women were more likely than men to have a democratic leadership style. The effect size was .22.

Esteem Support

Esteem support is defined as messages provided to enhance others' self-esteem, including perceptions and feelings surrounding their attributes, abilities, and accomplishments.[13] My colleagues from Michigan State[14] and I conducted an experiment to examine how both biological sex and gender influence the provision of esteem support messages. Additionally, my colleagues and I were interested in a potential interaction between one's own sex and the recipient's sex influencing esteem support messages. Regarding the provider's sex and gender, both women and those high in femininity indicated a greater likelihood of using the highest quality esteem support message, which is high emotion-focused messages (biological sex Cohen's d = .24 and gender's Cohen's d = .32). Consistently, both women and those high in femininity indicated a greater likelihood of using high problem-focused messages (biological sex Cohen's d = .23 and gender's Cohen's d = .29). However, no sex or gender differences emerged on low emotion-focused, low problem-focused, or messages containing no emotion and/or problem-focused content. When we interacted with the provider's sex with the recipient's sex, only one significant result emerged. Women providing esteem support to men indicated a greater likelihood of using highly problem-focused messages compared to men providing esteem support to other men (Cohen's d = .21). It is important to note that this study is not a meta-analysis like the previous ones, though this study was experimental in design.

12. Eagly and Johnson (1990) and Eagly et al. (1995).
13. Holmstrom and Burleson (2011).
14. Shebib et al. (2020).

Chapter Summary

- There are many myths about sex differences in communication.
- Men and women differ more in physical characteristics (ball throwing distance, $d = 1.98$; height, $d = 1.72$) and sexual things than in how they communicate.
- Most sex differences in communication are small ($d < .30$).

In the next chapter, Dr. Levine will discuss the work of the famous sociologist Irving Goffman and how his ideas help us understand human communication.

CHAPTER 17

Goffman and Self-Presentation

[Dr. Levine's Voice]

Returning to MSU as a professor was an odd experience for me, and it required more subtle social negotiation than I anticipated. I joined the faculty at MSU after 7 years in Hawaii and, prior to that, a 2-year stint as a visiting professor at Indiana University. I had been gone for almost a decade. When I left, I was still a graduate student. I returned as a tenured professor. My former professors were now my colleagues.

The weirdness stemmed from the differences between the me-in-graduate-school that the other professors had previously known and the professor-me that returned to MSU. I had changed quite a bit. They treated me as the old me—as the me they had known. I acted out the new me. This, of course, created a disconnect. The people I was interacting with daily were not on the same page with me regarding who I was. We were acting off different social scripts. It took about a year to work itself out. I persisted in being the then-current version of me, and gradually others began taking me as the person they were gradually coming to know in real time rather than the old me of their memories.

College students often have similar sorts of experiences. Students who go off to college may find themselves in a new social situation surrounded by people with whom they do not have prior interaction history. Being in a new social environment allows people to re-intent themselves if they want. Even if the reinvention is not intentional, being in new social situations offers opportunities for change and growth. In contrast, being around the same people can constrain us to being the same person. Students who go off to college are often surprised when they return home and see old friends. It can seem like the old social circle has not changed much and is out of sync with the returnee's view of themselves. A common feeling is of changing more than those in the old circle. That's how I felt in college when seeing my old high school friends over breaks. Of course, the opposite is also possible. People can see themselves as the same person as always while thinking that others have changed. The idea here is that there is how we see ourselves, how we act around others, how others see us, and how others act toward us. These can align or conflict, but all four affect how interactions play out.

Goffman

This chapter is about the works and ideas of the famed sociologist *Erving Goffman*. I consider knowing and understanding Goffman's perspective to be among the most essential foundations for understanding human communication. His work is up there in centrality and importance with Berlo and process or Cialdini's mechanisms of influence. It's absolutely bedrock. It also has a transformational quality, like learning Leon Festinger's theory of cognitive dissonance. Goffman's perspective changes your understanding of social interaction. Once you "get" Goffman, you see the world differently. Importantly for us, Goffman has much to say about how to be a competent communicator. Reading and rereading Goffman over the years has shaped my understanding of communication and made me a better communicator. His ideas have aged well. It is a body of work that has grown on me, and my appreciation for it has increased over time. It is as relevant now as ever, and the current me appreciates Goffman even more than earlier versions of me.

Interaction as Theater

When we are in the presence of others, we metaphorically step onto a stage with other actors and an audience. Often, we might be just the "extras" on the stage, just a person in the background or walking past. Whether we are an extra in a supporting role or the star of the show, we are playing the role of ourselves just as the others around us are playing themselves. This is Goffman's main metaphor. Interacting with others is like being an actor in a play. I find it useful to take the theatrical metaphor quasi-literally. I keep in mind that it is a metaphor, albeit a useful one.

When we are acting on the social stage of everyday life, how we play our role matters, just as it matters how others play their roles. For the production to come off well, everyone needs to play their part, and importantly, everyone needs to be reading from the same script. Imagine for a moment watching a stage production where one actor is playing a role from Star Wars, another actor is doing classic Shakespeare, a third is enacting a Broadway musical, while a fourth actor is doing a scene from a K-drama. The result would be nonsensical and beyond weird. The point is, it matters how the roles are played and how the roles fit together to form the arch of the story, the plot, and the subplots. Interaction requires coherence and coordination. The actors' roles and portrayals need to fit with each other, with the set and the props, and with the storyline. And this is a live-action stage play, not a film. We do not get multiple takes if we fumble our lines, and there is no way to edit gaffes out.

Maintaining the Expressive Order

When everything is working together, the **expressive order** is maintained. Everyone is playing their roles well enough, everyone knows their lines as well as the other actor's lines, the timing is working, and everyone is on the same page. The interaction goes smoothly, and nothing gets weird or awkward. Interaction flows and works for everyone. This, according to Goffman, is usually as it should be, how we all want it to be, and it is a worthy goal in its own right. Everyone works together to maintain the expressive order, and everyone benefits from things being well and good. Part of communication competence is playing your part in maintaining the expressive order. Violating the expressive order is cringe-inducing and is usually frowned upon.

Of course, sometimes we might purposely violate the expressive order. We might want to make a scene to make a point. Sometimes the expressive order does not work for everyone, and it needs to be disrupted. When the expressive order is disrupted, resistance and backlash can be expected. For example, at the start of Chapter 19, I will tell the story about leaving MSU for Korea University. I was in a play where I did not like parts of the storyline. I intentionally disrupted the expressive order to try to establish a better one. This was uncomfortable for me and others. People who were committed to the old expressive order tried to keep me in line and were frustrated that I was not playing along with their script. When I failed to change the expressive order, I moved on to take a role in a different theater troupe. I successfully auditioned to play myself at Korea University, and my role as a professor at MSU came to an end even more awkwardly than it started.

Self-Presentation and Impression Management

When we are in the actual or virtual presence of others, we are presenting who we are to other people, and they are forming impressions of us. Those impressions might be fleeting if you are barely noticed, or they can be more substantial. Sometimes, we are mindful of the impressions we are trying to create. Other times, we may not be aware of the impressions we are giving off and the impressions other people are forming of us. Others form impressions of us whether we want them to or not. So long as we are within the awareness of another person, an impression is possible.

Self-presentation is the process of giving off social information about ourselves to others. As I mentioned, it can be mindful, it can be strategic, or we can be unaware that we are doing so. When we are trying to create a particular impression, we can call this **impression management**. If you are just sitting at a coffee shop, you may not be thinking about how others might be seeing you. When we are interviewing for a job, in contrast, most of us will be very aware of how we are presenting ourselves and trying to mindfully give off the impression of someone who would be good to hire.

We have probably all heard about the power of first impressions, but impressions are not static. Just as communication is a process, so is giving off and making impressions. Impressions can be strong or weak, good or bad, more or less fluid, or anywhere in between. Regardless, whenever there is someone observing us, we are presenting ourselves.

Line, Face, FTAs, and Facework

In communication, Goffman might be best known for his work on the concept of *face*. If you take away one thing from this chapter, remember that face can be a big deal. Managing your own and other's face is an important part of being a competent communicator.

According to Goffman, when we are in social situations, we act out a **line**. Line is a broad concept. It includes how you are presenting yourself, but also the situation you take yourself to be in, who you think the others are who are also in the situation, and your stance toward them. You might, for example, present a different version of yourself at work than you do at school, thereby taking on different lines. We act differently at a coffee shop than we do at a concert and differently at an orchestral concert than at a hip-hop concert. We treat friends differently than strangers. How we interact conveys who we are, where we are, what we are doing, and who we are with. This is our line.

Lines have a social inertia to them. Once we start a line, others will orient toward that line and treat that as our line. Goffman points out that people might not be mindful of their lines, but from the perspective of those around us, people are presumed to choose their lines and are expected to follow through with them. You do not get to change characters or roles in the middle of an act.

People also have a face. **Face** is *the positive social value people claim for themselves through their lines*. Your face involves the positive image you convey to others because you are playing the role of a good character, playing your role well, and doing your part to maintain the expressive order. You can think of your face as your good name or your reputation.

To have face, you need to take a good line, keep the line consistent, and have the line supported by others. To play our role well, others need to cooperate and be in sync with us. For example, when I play Professor Levine in lecture, my role and performance depend on students accepting me in my role and playing the roles of Professor Levine's students. Me coming off well in my role (and me having face) requires others to play along. Of course, it works both ways. I need to support my students in their roles. That way, everyone gets their face. Think of it as being mutually respectful.

People *lose face* when information is brought about that is inconsistent with their line. This can happen when a person is presenting themselves one way, but it is clear to those around them that that is not who they are. We can lose face when we do not present a consistent line. We can also lose face when others challenge our face. Others may just not play along, or worse, they can be antagonistic or insulting. Big disruptions to the expressive order can make everyone lose face.

Sometimes people just do not know what line to take. This can happen when you are in a new situation and you do not know how you should act. Goffman calls this being *out of face*.

Anything that might harm a person's face, causing them to lose face, is called a *face threat*. A *face-threatening act*, or FTA, then, is an action that might harm someone's face. People who do FTAs can be seen as rude or as a "jerk." Of course, sometimes FTAs cannot be helped. Sometimes we must do things that might hurt someone's feelings or make them look bad. As a department chair, I have had to write negative performance reviews. But FTAs should not be done for the purpose of being face threatening. Malicious, mean-spirited FTAs are especially bad.

People's face is important to them. No one likes to lose face, and people do not appreciate threats to their own face. This said, people (and cultures) also differ in how face-sensitive they are. Some people will lash out when their face is threatened. Some people hold grudges.

People typically find observing face threats to others uncomfortable. People, however, also differ in their sensitivity to other's faces. If you see someone embarrassed, how bad do you feel for them? Do you cover your face with your hands, close your eyes, and wince?

Facework is any action done to mitigate face threats. Being *polite* helps prevent face threats or responding to them once they occur. For example, people might apologize.

Managing self and others' face sets up **Goffman's twin rules of interaction**. The first rule is to practice **self-respect**. Act in a way that is consistent with your face, and avoid threatening your own face. To do this, you need to pick a good line and play it through. Choose the roles you play well. Present yourself favorably and consistently.

The second rule is **considerateness**. Let other people have their face. Do not needlessly threaten other people's faces. Act out your line in such a way that others also have good lines to take as well. If you notice others are struggling with their lines, help them out.

The trick, of course, is balancing the twin rules and acting in accordance with both at the same time. You come away looking good; others look good too. Everyone keeps face. The expressive order is maintained. Social functioning is smooth. No one feels or looks awkward. Nothing is cringeworthy. This can be easier said than done sometimes, but a hallmark of good, competent communication is making it so.

Cooling the Mark

Social interactions are not always smooth for everyone. Sometimes difficult conversations are unavoidable. Some situations are highly face threatening by their very nature. Sometimes people lose face. In such situations, we need damage control. We want to prevent people who have lost face from lashing out and to minimize the forming and holding of grudges.

One of my favorite Goffman essays is on *cooling the mark out*. The essay shifts the metaphor from the theater to the world of crime, scams, and conmen. The mark is the victim of the scam, and the operators are the criminals running the con or scam. Goffman points out that being scammed is doubly painful for the mark. There is the material cost of what they got scammed out of but also there is the embarrassment of falling for the scam. Marks do not want to see themselves as gullible and as the sort of person who would allow themselves to be so victimized. Falling for a scam means losing face.

It is in the criminal's interest for the mark to accept their loss and move on. They do not want the mark to go to the police, report the crime, or try to get revenge. That is bad for their criminal business. So, they will try to cool the mark out. Cooling the mark out refers to things the criminals do to facilitate an exit and preempt avoidable fallout from actions.

Goffman uses cooling the mark as a metaphor for dealing with a variety of noncriminal, everyday situations where someone gets their face threatened, and someone else (the "cooler") tries to get them to chill, thereby minimizing potential disruption to the expressive order.

In my MSU example at the beginning of the chapter on fairness, MSU's inability to cool me out resulted in me leaving, harboring resentments, and ultimately hiring away some of their more valuable faculty to come work for me at UAB. Cooling the mark out, or not, can have high stakes. Being a good communicator requires recognizing the need for cooling and knowing how to cool someone out when needed.

Examples in which someone might need to be cooled are numerous. A customer service agent dealing with an irate customer needs to cool the customer out. Giving someone a bad grade or a poor performance evaluation may require some cooling. So might breaking up with a romantic partner.

There are many strategies available for cooling a mark out, but they all depend on the situation. If a professor in my department is having a particularly difficult time dealing with a student who is upset about a grade, they might call me in as the chair. Bringing in someone of higher status or more organizational power is a cooling strategy. In my role as cooler-in-chief for the department, I have multiple communication goals. I need to be sure university policies are followed. I need to be sure that principles of fairness are upheld. But also, if possible, I want to contain the situation and "handle" it at my level. When problems move up the chain of command, by definition, it signals that things are not running smoothly and that I am not handling them sufficiently well to avoid the involvement of higher-ups. For these reasons, cooling skills are critical for all people in an organizational hierarchy, whether in their official job description or not.

A common cooling strategy is allowing someone to vent. Being vented at is no fun, but often, those who are venting will run out of steam. Feeling "heard" and understood is socially healing. Showing empathy is usually a good move. Sometimes providing advice is not the best way to go. Just listen and understand the person's perspective.

Because a person who needs to be cooled out has lost face, many cooling strategies involve providing ways for them to save face. Maybe a person who is going to be fired can be allowed to resign. Maybe they can get some consolation prize. Maybe it can be communicated that what is happening is not their fault. The best cooling strategy, however, is prevention. Faces that are not threatened do not need to be saved.

Chapter Summary

- Goffman uses a theatrical metaphor to understand interaction. We play the role of ourselves, and other people play themselves.
- When interacting, there is an **expressive order** to maintain. Disruptions to the expressive order are uncomfortable.

- **Face** is the positive social image people have. Good communication involves self-respect (having one's own face) and considerateness (others having their face).
- When another person's face is threatened, we may need to cool them out.

Next up, Dr. Shebib discusses the important topics of attributions, uncertainty, and uncertainty reduction.

CHAPTER 18

Uncertainty and Attributions

[*Dr. Shebib's Voice*]

P eople have a strong need to understand the question "why" because it helps us to understand the world around us. This is especially true of our social world. We wonder why people are doing what they do. When we understand why people do what they do, we can better anticipate what they will do, and we can better know how best to interact with them. When we don't know why someone did something, we are uncertain, and we want to reduce that uncertainty. The explanations we create for why people did something are called *attributions*.

Every day, we make attributions, often subconsciously and without awareness about why things happen or why people do what they do. We even make attributions to explain why we behave a certain way or why something happened to us the way it did. For example, when we get a poor grade on an exam or an assignment, we might blame the professor for not teaching the right material in the lecture. When a friend or a classmate gets a better grade on that same exam or assignment, we might attribute their good grade to better testing skills than ourselves or even to luck. We make attributions all the time, and they influence how we feel and how we relate to people around us.

Attribution Theory

Attribution theory is a set of theories that provide us with ways to describe and understand how people answer the question "why." Attribution theory is based on the idea that people make sense of their social world by identifying the causes of the behaviors they observe and the events they experience. Ascribing causes is the core of attribution theory. The primary causes for behavior can be internal, external, or intentional. Most older attribution theories focus on the first two—internal and external attributions—so I will start with these.

In most versions of attribution theory, when we decide why people act the way they do, our explanations fall into one of two broad categories: either the person or the situation. An **internal (or dispositional or personal) attribution** is made by deciding the cause of their behavior is due to some stable characteristic of the person. This can include things like personality. Why did they do that thing? That is just the way they are. On the other hand, an **external (or situational) attribution** is made by deciding that the cause of their behavior is due to something in the situation or the environment.

Let's take, for example, me observing a student arriving late to class. I can make one of two attributions. An internal (dispositional) attribution would be this student is not very conscientious and doesn't care about my class or about being on time. On the other hand, I could make an external (situational) attribution and think this student must have gotten stuck in traffic or could not find parking.

The actor-observer hypothesis states that people tend to explain their own behavior with situational causes and other people's behavior with personal causes. This asymmetry is often described as a firmly established fact.

However, a meta-analysis[1] of 173 published studies revealed that research does not actually support this. The actor-observer hypothesis only holds for negative events. The reverse asymmetry happens for positive events. When something good happens, we take credit for it. For negative events, people tend to explain their own behavior with situational causes and other people's behavior with internal causes. But for positive events, people tend to explain their own behavior with internal causes and other people's behavior with situational causes. This is sometimes called *self-serving attributions*.

A psychologist named Bertram Malle argues that internal and external attributions apply to behaviors that are unintended and do not work as well for behaviors that are intentional. Thus, applying the previous example, someone who cannot help themselves and is often late for things (a dispositional reason) or a person stuck in traffic (situational reason) is not trying to be late. Malle proposes that for intentional things people are purposefully doing, we make **reason explanations**. These are people's explanations of intentional behavior that cite the person's reasons for acting intentionally. So, for example, if someone decided (decisions being intentional) not to come to class, we might look for their reasons. Reasons lead to intentions, and intentions lead to actions. For example, Dr. Levine and I decided to write this book. The answer to why we chose to do it involves identifying our reasons. Can you guess our reasons?

Attributions and Communication

Attributions shape how we approach and respond to other people. It's important to understand, though, that **the attributions we make are not always accurate**. They can be accurate, partially correct, or simply inaccurate. So, it's always best to have conversations to understand the situation and behaviors of another person before allowing your perceived attribution to explain the entire situation. This of this as the "don't jump to conclusions" rule of competent communication.

Uncertainty and Uncertainty Reduction Theory (URT)

Our experience of the world is intimately linked to our level of uncertainty. When we receive information that reduces uncertainty, we are more confident that we understand ourselves, other people, our relationships, and the world around us. In most cases, the more information we have about someone, the more we feel we know that person. A lack of information, or information that violates expectations, often increases uncertainty.

In social situations, **uncertainty** can be defined as *the inability to predict or explain* someone's attitudes and/or behaviors. More broadly, researchers argue that uncertainty occurs when people feel insecure in their own state of knowledge or the state of knowledge in general about a topic. When we define uncertainty in social situations, it is important to highlight that uncertainty encompasses an inability to do two things: (a) predict someone's behavior and (b) explain someone's behavior. We want to be able to both **predict and explain** someone's behavior; thus, we want to reduce uncertainty.

URT focuses on understanding what happens during initial interactions when two people meet.[2] URT maintains that the driving force in initial encounters is obtaining information about the other person to get

1. Jones and Nisbett (1971).
2. Berger and Calabrese (1975).

to know her or him better and, ultimately, to reduce uncertainty. The theory offers 7 general predictions and 21 more specific predictions. My focus here, however, is on three general issues that provided a foundation for the theory and spawned later research: (1) the motivation to reduce uncertainty, (2) the relationship between communication and uncertainty, and (3) the ways people use communication to strategically to reduce uncertainty.

One of the primary principles underlying URT was that people generally dislike uncertainty and are therefore motivated to reduce it. Scholars have argued that our reason for behaving the way we do during initial interactions with strangers is simple: we want to get to know them better. Not only do we *want* to get to know them, but we *must* get to know them better so that we can reduce uncertainty and create order in our world. The more we can reduce uncertainty, the better we can accomplish our goals. In other words, we dislike situations in which we are unsure about the outcome; we do our best to create predictable environments, and it is in our interests to do so.

Strategies for Reducing Uncertainty

URT also suggests that people communicate in strategic ways to reduce uncertainty. Specifically, researchers identified three general ways people go about reducing uncertainty in initial encounters: passive strategies, active strategies, and interactive strategies.

Passive Strategies

People who rely on unobtrusive observation are using ***passive strategies***.[3] These strategies involve behaviors such as looking at someone sitting alone to see if a friend or date comes along, observing how a person interacts with others, or paying attention to the kinds of clothes a person wears. Based on observation, you might make assumptions about someone's age, relational status (e.g., is the person physically close to the other individual? Is someone wearing a ring?), and personality, among many other characteristics. Passive observations are likely to be effective and informative when they are conducted in an informal setting, like a party, rather than in a formal setting, like a classroom or business office. People usually make more accurate judgments when watching someone interact with others than when the person is sitting alone. Most people's communication is constrained in formal settings because rules in these situations are fairly strict, so their behavior is not particularly informative. By contrast, people act in unique, personal ways at an informal party or in many online settings because the "rules" are less rigid. Therefore, it is more informative and, consequently, much more uncertainty reducing to observe someone in an informal, as opposed to a formal, setting. Unfortunately, there's also a dark side to passive uncertainty reduction: When passive observation strategies become compulsive, stalking or relational intrusion is the result.

Active Strategies

The second strategy is an ***active strategy***,[2] and it can take one of two forms. One type involves ***manipulating***

3. Berger (1979, 1987).

the social environment and then observing how someone reacts. The information seeker may not be part of the manipulated situation, although he or she sets up the situation. These tactics are like mini experiments conducted with the intent of gaining information about the target person. For example, several students in my classes have admitted using active uncertainty reduction strategies with dating partners (e.g., flirting with someone else to see how their partner reacts) or leaving their relational partner alone with a flirtatious friend to see what the partner would do.

The second type of active uncertainty reduction strategy involves **asking third parties** (i.e., friends, family members) about the person in question. We often ask friends if they have heard anything about a particular person of interest or ask for help interpreting something that person did. In fact, one study[4] found that 30% of the information we have about someone comes from asking others.

Interactive Strategies

The third general type of uncertainty reduction strategy is interactive. **Interactive strategies** involve direct contact between the information seeker and the target. Common interactive strategies include asking questions, encouraging disclosure, and relaxing the target. We are especially likely to ask such questions the first time we meet someone. In studies of behavior during initial interactions, researchers have found that the frequency of question-asking drops over time, coinciding with decreases in our level of uncertainty.[5] It is important to note, though, that the questions being asked in initial interactions are usually very general. Research suggests that we hesitate to ask questions about intimate issues until we have a close relationship with the person and, even then, may avoid asking direct questions.[6]

Secret Tests

Relational scholars examine things that people do to reduce uncertainty in close relationships and refer to them as *secret tests*. According to research,[7] there are at least seven strategies people can use to reduce their uncertainty about their partner's commitment to the relationship.

The first is the **asking-third-party test**. This strategy relies on feedback from social network members. "Facebook creeping" is an example of asking a third party.

The second is the **directness test**. This strategy involves talking about issues with the partner and includes strategies such as asking questions and discussing things the person feels uncertain about. This test is like the interactive strategies described earlier. Unlike the other "secret" tests here, this strategy involves direct communication.

Third is the **triangle test**. This strategy is intended to test the partner's commitment to the relationship by creating three-person triangles. Fidelity checks (such as seeing if the partner responds to a fictitious "secret admirer" note) and jealousy tests (such as flirting with someone else to see how the partner responds) are two

---

4. Hewes et al. (1985).

5. Douglas (1990) and Kellermann (1995).

6. Bell and Buerkel-Rothfuss (1990).

7. All secret test(s) information comes from Baxter and Wilmot (1984).

examples of triangle tests. There's a TikTok account, @aye_its_emilyy, that conducts triangle tests on people's partners who ask her to! Check them out; they are quite interesting!

Fourth is the **separation test**. This strategy relies on creating physical distance between relational partners by long periods of physical separation or by ceasing contact for an extended period to see how long it takes for your partner to call.

Fifth is the **endurance test**. This strategy increases the costs or reduces the rewards for the other person in the relationship. One such test, known as "testing limits," involves seeing how much a partner will endure.

Sixth is the **public presentation test**. This strategy involves monitoring a partner's reaction to the use of certain relational labels or actions. It is most used in early relationship stages. Public presentation tests that might occur later in the relationship include engagement rings, for example.

Finally, seventh is the **indirect suggestion test**. This strategy uses hints or jokes to bring up a topic without taking responsibility. The partner's response provides insight into her or his feelings about the issue.

Chapter Summary

- People need to understand their social world and are motivated to do so.
- Attributions are perceived causes of and explanations for behaviors.
- Attributions can be internal (dispositional), external (situational), or intentional (reasons).
- When we cannot predict and explain things, we are uncertain, and we will seek to reduce the uncertainty.
- Reducing uncertainty is one of the functions of communication, and we can do this through passive, active, and interactive strategies.

In the next chapter, Dr. Levine will discuss fairness.

CHAPTER 19

Fairness and Equity

[Dr. Levine's Voice]

One big reason I left MSU was a perception of a lack of fairness. The professors in my department were not all treated fairly. I came to believe that there was a dysfunctional culture of favoritism and a lack of equity. Personally, I was treated very well. But I observed that others were not, and it created a toxic work environment. Unfortunately, not everyone agreed that there was a problem that needed fixing. Some of the people I worked with flat-out denied the concerns I expressed. When it became apparent that fixing the situation was beyond my ability, it was time to move on.

Now, as a department chair, I have both the responsibility and the social power to create a work environment that is inclusive, fair, and just. I see this as the sine qua non (absolutely necessary; literally without which, not) of effective leadership and healthy, functional social relations. It, however, is not enough to treat others fairly. **Fairness needs to be communicated and mutually recognized. People need to feel like they are being treated fairly.**

One of the iron laws of social situations is that being **treated unfairly really pisses people off**. It is incontrovertible that perceptions of unfairness inexorably lead to anger and resentment. It follows that not only do we need to treat others fairly, but also that we convey that fairness in how we communicate. The consequences of doing otherwise are socially toxic. We all need to work toward fairness for all to create an environment where competent communication can take place.

Before we know how to incorporate being fair and communicating that fairness into our communication skill set, we need to know what fairness is and how to achieve it. This is a bit tricky because there are different approaches to fairness. **Not everyone sees fairness through the same lens.**

Three Approaches to Fairness

Let me tell you about the compensation systems at the different universities where I have been a professor. You may or may not have an interest in how professor salaries are determined, but they do exemplify critical aspects of fairness and thus serve as good examples for our discussion. As I am describing them, ask yourself these three questions: (1) Which system do you prefer, (2) which is the fairest, and (3) why did you answer the previous questions as you did?

At the University of Hawaii, salaries were on a step system. Starting salaries were negotiable, but once you were at a given salary step, your raises were fixed and the same as everyone else's. In years when there were raises, either everyone moved up a step or the pay associated with each step moved up some fixed amount. So, for example, everyone who was a step 3 assistant professor would get the same raise regardless of performance or market forces unique to a person or academic field.

At Korea University, there was a similar system with three differences. First, starting salaries were not negotiable and were based on prior experience. All the full professors with 10 years in rank, for example, made the same salary. Unlike Hawaii, however, step raises were tied to performance evaluations. A minimum level of performance on a highly quantified set of metrics was required to get a step raise. In Hawaii, everyone who was still employed got a step raise when available; in Korea, you could keep your job but miss a raise if your performance did not meet the minimum expectation. Everyone who met the minimum was treated the same. Third, there were performance-based bonuses available, but those were one-time payments and did not affect one's base salary.

At MSU, starting salaries were negotiable, and raises were all merit based. That is, all raises were tied to performance evaluations. Further, additional "super-merit" was possible where unusually high performance in a year could lead to a merit-on-top-of-merit raise. Over a 10-year span, salaries of individual professors could double, remain essentially unchanged, or be a more typical 20%–30% increase. Counteroffer raises matching or exceeding offers from other universities were also common and sometimes offered preemptively. Thus, applying to other universities every few years was a second way to boost one's salary. This created huge differences in compensation between coworkers, and the people with the most seniority were among the highest and the lowest paid professors within the same department.

UAB has merit raises, too, but the system is more constrained than at MSU, limiting the extreme differences in raises that were possible at MSU. There is also a system at UAB for looking at unfair differences in salaries so underpaid professors can get their compensation back in line with their peers.

Now that the four systems have been summarized, what are your thoughts?

Hawaii and Korea are examples of **equality** approaches to fairness. In an equality approach, the basic rule is to treat everyone the same. In a pure equality system, resources are evenly distributed among all. Fairness means no favoritism and no discrimination. Everyone has the same rights, privileges, and restrictions. Everyone doing the same job gets paid the same.

MSU and UAB, in contrast, are examples of **equity** approaches. In equity approaches, people get what they deserve and deserve what they get. Equity approaches are *meritocratic*. For example, better performing employees get bigger raises. You must pay someone who is more marketable a higher salary to keep them. High performance is incentivized.

Of course, most systems have aspects of both equality and equity approaches in varying degrees.

My guess is that most readers think they prefer an equity approach to an equality approach. People like to be rewarded for their hard work and tangible personal successes. People usually like the idea of having the chance to get ahead of others by working hard, being diligent, accumulating accomplishments, or just having natural talent. This seems right and feels good. If I am right about this, the MSU merit system is the most attractive, and the Hawaii system is the least appealing to many readers. So then, will MSU attract and keep the best people? Does the Hawaii system encourage free-riding and, over time, result in lower faculty performance?

In my opinion, Hawaii's system did create problems, but not the ones you might expect. I did not observe much loafing there, and the lack of competition encouraged cooperation. The problem was the inflexibility of the system to deal with external competition from other universities. The University of Hawaii lost much talent because other universities paid better, especially in comparison to the cost of living. MSU's system created problems of a different sort. Big inequities emerged over time, creating resentment and a contentious work environment. In practice, MSU failed to retain many high performers even with their merit system. MSU was good for my paychecks, but I like(d) working in the Korea University and UAB systems better because they offer a better balance of equity and equality. In terms of faculty retention, Korea University and UAB had much less turnover than the University of Hawaii or MSU.

Equality Systems

As I mentioned, the principle of equality is to treat people the same. Equal protection under the law is an equality-based idea, as are flat taxes and antidiscrimination policies. When I apply the same grading system or rubrics to everyone in a class, I am practicing an equality approach to fairness. My parents applied this approach at Christmas for my brother and me. We always received gifts of approximately the same value.

Equity Systems

Equity systems, in contrast, seek to provide outcomes proportional to performance or contribution. For example, when I evaluate one student's paper as higher quality than another's paper, the better paper should get a better grade. That is fair. If you bring in more profit for your company, you should get paid better. More qualifications or experience should lead to a higher salary.

Although equity systems are appealing, there are at least three challenges to making an equity system fair in practice. First, there can be issues in defining and assessing performance or contribution. In grading a student paper, what makes a good paper good? The choice of rubrics used can be subjective and favor some students over others. In evaluating professors, do we judge teaching or research as more important? What, for example, counts as evidence of instructional quality? Second, maintaining proportionality can be tricky. It is one thing to accept the principle that a better paper should get a higher grade, but how much better is one paper than another, and how much better grade does it get? To be fair, proportionality is required, but it is not always clear how to create or ensure proportionality. Finally, merit systems can only be fair where there is equality of opportunity for merit. For example, consider using test scores as methods for selecting students for admission to college. Tests are fair if everyone has the same chance to prepare for them and to do well. If the tests have some cultural or social bias, or if some test-takers have some advantage (being from an affluent family who can afford the best tutors), then it might not be a fair playing field.

Procedural Justice

The third approach to fairness is the idea of procedural justice. The idea is to set up clear and transparent policies and then to apply them evenly. This might include policies for grade disputes or to adjudicate allegations of academic dishonesty. They often include mechanisms for an appeal process.

Psychological Contracts

When people come to formal, legally binding agreements, they may sign a contract. For example, I have an employment contract with UAB. It specifies my duties and things I should and should not do. It also specifies UAB's obligations to me. When Dr. Shebib and I started this book, we signed a contract with the publisher. Contracts of these sorts are formal and explicit. All parties entering the contract should know what they agree to, and what they agree to is explicitly spelled out.

Psychological contracts are more informal understandings and expectations. They are unwritten. These are things that people think are agreed upon. For example, in a class, the syllabus serves as a more formal contract. But professors have expectations of students that go beyond what appears in the syllabus, just as students have expectations for classes and professors that go beyond the syllabus and formal university policies. Some things are just understood or presumed to be understood. There is a tacit agreement. The point is, **when people feel like a psychological contract has been broken, they can experience that as unfairness**. It feels like a broken promise or a bait and switch. We need to be aware of psychological contracts, keep them realistic, and honor them if possible.

Confronting Unfairness

Confronting unfairness has, as communication goes, a high degree of difficulty. As I mentioned and cannot stress enough, people do not appreciate the unfairness directed at them. The natural reaction to experiencing unfairness is anger. Anger makes people want to lash out. Repressed anger builds into resentment over time. These are socially unhealthy. Anger aside, people who experience unfairness want it to be recognized and acknowledged. They often want an apology from the offending party; they may want compensation for past wrongs; perhaps most of all, they want the situation to improve. They want to be treated more fairly moving forward, and they want the system changed so others do not go through what they did.

Many times, the main obstacle to remedying unfairness is defensiveness by the party being accused of being unfair. People treating others unfairly will often deny the existence of unfairness and see the accusation as an insult. This puts the person being treated unfairly in a bind. Trying to fix the situation just results in being gaslit. There is pushback. It is hard to fix a problem that is not acknowledged, and the lack of recognition makes the situation worse. I wish I had some magic wand for the victims of unfairness, but the truth is, it can be difficult to get past the defensiveness to achieve a fair solution. It is good to be aware of the potential for denial and pushback. Just because others will not acknowledge the situation does not mean that it is not real.

Because of this difficulty in confronting unfairness, the best thing to do is to prevent it in the first place. Recognize the importance of perception of fairness in social functioning. Understand the different approaches to fairness and apply them to situations in ways that make sense. Seek transparency and clarity. When people express feelings of unfairness, hear them out. Practice perspective taking. Cooperate on solutions. Actively work toward social situations where there is a consensus that things are fair and where there are mechanisms in place to restore fairness if needed.

Chapter Summary

- No one likes to be treated unfairly. Perceptions of unfairness lead to anger and resentment and impede good communication and healthy relationships.
- **Part of being a good communicator is not only treating others fairly but also conveying fairness so that it is felt and shared by everyone.**
- Equality involves treating everyone the same.
- Equity is when outcomes are proportional to inputs or what is deserved. It is a merit-based approach.
- Procedural justice involves clear and transparent rules for achieving fairness.
- Confronting unfairness is difficult because allegations of unfairness are often met with defensiveness and pushback. Denying the validity of felt unfairness makes things worse.

Next up, I will talk about theory of mind and empathy. Both are essential for communication.

CHAPTER 20

Theory of Mind and Empathy

[*Dr. Levine's Voice*]

Times have changed. As an undergraduate student, all the classes in my major were graded on a curve. There was no set-in-advance score total or percentage for a particular grade. What mattered was how well a student did relative to the other students in the class. Scores near the average were Cs, and about half the students in the class got a C. To get an A, you needed to be in the top 5%, preferably with a "cut-point" (i.e., gap) between you and the next highest score. In a class with 30 or 40 students, only the top student or two could get As. A 75% could be an A so long as everyone else did worse. A 95% might not be an A if several students scored over 90%.

In hindsight, I think this was a terrible way to grade. It fostered competitiveness rather than cooperation. At the time, however, it was just how it was. If you wanted good grades (and I did), you just had to consistently score at the top of each class.

Having a high grade point average in that grading system required more than just learning the material, although knowing the material inside out was essential. To get an advantage, I practiced what I called "psych the professor." This involved knowing what the professor thought was important, figuring out what the professor was looking for or getting at, and trying to see the professor's perspective on the test or assignment. I'd do my best to get into the professor's head. I'd pay attention to which topics they spent the most time on and any editorializing they did. I picked up on their quirks and idiosyncrasies and adapted accordingly. That skill set has served me well in life. Being socially perceptive and socially adaptive is advantageous.

In the final chapter, Dr. Shebib and I will summarize how to be good at communication. In the field of communication, I see two approaches to understanding communication competence. The more common approach focuses on *messages* and looks at what is said independently from the specific people who are communicating. This view presumes that there are better and worse things to say in a situation. In contrast, my view is that one size does not fit all. There is no one or fixed right thing to say in situations of one kind or another. Communication needs to balance your being who you are and to tailor your communication to the person you are interacting with, given the situation at the time. Doing that requires understanding the person you are interacting with.

Let's switch metaphors and think about gift-giving. Some gifts are just nicer than others. A nice watch is almost always a better gift than a pair of socks. But the best gifts are something that the receiver of the gift wants or needs, and they reflect thoughtfulness and insight into the recipient's perspective. The best gift for one person is not the best gift for someone else. The best communication is like this too. It is adapted to the audience and the circumstances.

Here is another personal example to make the point. The first time I applied to be a professor at MSU, I was unsuccessful. The rejection letter read: "Dear Professor Levine, we had a number of good candidates. Unfortunately, you were not among them." Ouch! (at least on a surface reading). This rejection seems horribly insensitive and insulting. It was signed by the chair of the search committee, Dr. Franklin J. Boster. Frank was my

PhD advisor and major professor. Of course, I was disappointed with the outcome and would have been regardless of the wording in the letter. But I found the letter hilarious. People who did not know us might find the letter horrifying. The letter, however, worked, given the people and the context. Boster had supported me for the job. I knew that. The letter had a subtext that he knew I would get and appreciate. I am not recommending that you ever write a letter like that, but I do believe that communication is better if it is tailored to the individual. This kind of tailoring requires understanding other people. That is the central idea of this chapter.

Theory of Mind (TOM)

Communication requires *theory of mind*. The theory in TOM isn't a theory in a formal academic sense. URT, truth-default theory, and dissonance theories are examples of names of academic theories. In contrast, the theory part of TOM is more of a reference to a basic abstract understanding. TOM involves grasping the basic idea of "mind," that people have minds, and that people have their own minds different from the minds of others. People think things. People feel things. People want this or that. People have desires, goals, and perspectives. People have their own take on things. People think different things and see things differently than others. TOM is the mental ability to grasp the idea that other people can have something in mind and that what is in their mind can be different than what is on our mind. When I talked about "psyching the professor," that involved TOM. Understanding another person requires TOM, as does understanding how people can misunderstand each other.

Human children develop TOM early in childhood, but there is no exact age. Most 2-year-old children do not have it yet, but by age 7, most children do. TOM, however, is not an on-off, have-lack sort of thing. TOM can be more or less sophisticated. It generally gets more sophisticated with age, but people who are the same age can differ in TOM.

A common test of TOM goes something like this: I save a draft of this chapter in a cloud folder I share with Dr. Shebib. Unknown to me, when I am offline, she moves it to a different folder. When I come back online to work on the chapter, where will I look for it? Will I look for it where I saved it, or will I look for it where it is? I hope the answer is obvious. I will look for the document where I left it because that is where I think it will be. I didn't know that it was moved until I found it missing from where I thought I had saved it. However, those who have not developed TOM might answer differently. Knowing where I will look requires knowing what I do and do not know. That requires understanding things from my perspective and knowing that I can't know what Dr. Shebib did.

Empathy

Empathy is crucial for competent communication. Yet, empathy as a term and a concept is ambiguous because it can mean different things. I think of empathy as an umbrella term that can mean at least three different things: empathic concern, perspective taking, and emotional contagion.

Empathic concern means caring about others. People who have lots of empathic concern are people we think of as kind and caring. They want good things for other people, they tend to be helpful, and they feel bad (have sympathy for others) when they know other people are having difficulties.

Perspective taking is a second aspect or type of empathy. It involves understanding another person's point of view. If you can understand how one person might see something one way while another person can see the same thing differently, you are engaging in perspective taking. I think of perspective taking as a core social perception skill. Being good at social perception means understanding other people and social situations. Perspective taking is part of being socially perceptive.

Emotional contagion involves feeling what someone else is experiencing. The idea is *human emotions are contagious*. If you are around people who are happy, you are more likely to be happy. If people around you are excited, you might get excited. If someone is angry, you might get angry.

My former professors Jim Stiff and Kathy Miller, along with my friend Jim Dillard and some at-the-time graduate students, did a series of studies linking the various aspects of empathy with communication and social outcomes. They did a series of studies that produced some coherent and important results. What follows is an integration of their findings.

They found that perspective taking drives empathic concern. People who consider the perspectives of others tend to care more about others. In contrast, people less adept at perspective taking tend to score lower on empathic concern.

Empathic concern, in turn, leads to some desirable social outcomes and some drawbacks. On the upside, it makes people more responsive communicators. That is, perspective taking and caring more directly help tailor communication to whom you are interacting with. Empathic concern is generally linked with helping other people and with good communication skills. In short, the more you understand other people's perspectives, the more you care about other people, and this enables you to say things that work well for the situation. Interactions go better.

The downside of perspective taking is that it increases emotional contagion, which, unlike empathic concern and perspective taking, can be detrimental. To explain this, consider the example of someone working in customer service who is dealing with an irate customer. The customer is mad about something; the anger is being directed at the customer service agent. The customer service agent needs to resolve the situation. In the language of Chapter 17 on Goffman, the mark needs cooling out. Here is where emotional contagion can make a problem worse. If the customer service agent catches the customer's anger and responds back in kind, the situation gets heated, not cooled.

The communication trick is not letting other people's anger piss you off. That is, emotional contagion needs to be tamped down for negative emotions. Instead, you need to reverse engineer the emotional contagion which flows both ways. While anger directed at you tends to make you angry in return, directing calmness and respect back tends to cool the other person's anger. It is hard to be mad at someone who is nice, polite, and understanding.

The research found that the more people experienced emotional contagion, the less well they communicated, and the more likely they were to get burned out in their jobs. Thus, the take-home messages from the research were that people benefited from empathic concern and perspective taking. Those made them better communicators. People, however, needed to sever the link between empathic concern and emotional contagion. They need to understand others care about others but not get emotionally involved. This puts them in charge of the emotional tone, reduces negative emotions, and reduces stress for everyone.

Strategically lowering emotional contagion is difficult. Practice helps. When people do things that bother you, practice telling yourself things like "other people don't control my emotions," and "I don't give other people the power to ruin my day."

Chapter Summary

- TOM involves understanding the concept of the human mind.
- Empathy can be divided into three types: empathic concern, perspective taking, and emotional

contagion.
- Perspective taking involves understanding other's viewpoints and perspectives, and it leads to empathic concern.
- Empathic concern is being a caring person, and while it improves communication, it can also increase emotional contagion.
- Emotional contagion involves catching others' emotions and can interfere with competent communication.

Next up, I will talk about the important topic of communication networks.

CHAPTER 21

Networks

[*Dr. Levine's Voice*]

My first real professor job was at the University of Hawaii. I was a professor there for 7 years until I left to take a job at MSU. I really liked living in Hawaii. I like Asian food, and Hawaii has fantastic and authentic Chinese, Japanese, and Korean foods. While living there, I became a big fan of sushi and dim sum. Hawaii also has incredible weather. Once you get used to it, it is never too hot and never too cold. None of my apartments in Honolulu had heat or air conditioning. I just opened the windows and turned on a fan in summer and closed them in winter. Hawaii has incredible scenic beauty. I also like the people in Hawaii. I liked the students. I liked the people I worked with. I liked the diversity. The only things I don't miss are the high cost of living there and the long flights to and from Hawaii.

I learned about the job opening at the University of Hawaii before the job was publicly advertised. The department chair there, Michael Miller, had reached out to my advisor, Frank Boster, and Boster told me about it. I was an MSU graduate, and Michael Miller had been on the faculty at MSU before Hawaii. We both did our master's degrees at WVU, although not at the same time, we knew many of the same people. Two professors at Hawaii were also MSU grads (Rodney Reynolds and Min Sun Kim), and two more (Kelly and Krystyna Aune) were University of Arizona graduates who studied under former MSU faculty. I had many indirect connections to my future department. I think that probably gave me an advantage in getting hired there.

At the University of Hawaii, I began to fully appreciate the importance of networks in a way I had not previously. Many things there got done behind the scenes. To know what was going on and to have influence, it was essential to be well-connected with others at the university. Much of this happened at social gatherings rather than at work, a pattern I later recognized in Korean work life. Additionally, I worked in a small department, one of two communication departments on campus. There was a real concern we might be seen as redundant and be disbanded. To preempt this, we all got on every university committee we could and made a strategic effort to be well-known, highly regarded, and liked around campus. It worked.

Jumping ahead to UAB, I got invited to apply at UAB because someone here knew someone who knew me. Similarly, I got into my master's program at WVU at least in part because one of my professors at Northern Arizona University knew Jim McCroskey, who was chair at WVU. I got into MSU for my PhD, at least in part because of letters from McCroskey, Wheeless, and Richmond. I got hired in Korea because they were recruiting my wife. See the trend? Establishing and maintaining networks matters.

While a student at MSU, I took a seminar from Professor Mac Parks that changed how I understood communication. The idea was that viewing communication in terms of the relationship between the people interacting misses an important aspect of the bigger picture. All communication is embedded in larger communication networks. Communication between friends is part of a larger circle of friends. Communication between coworkers or students exists within organizational and school networks. Communication with a family member is part of a larger family network. Further, these various networks can overlap and intertwine.

Communication Networks

Our **communication networks** consist of the people we communicate with, the people those we communicate with communicate with, who they communicate with, and on out. The people we interact with are our *direct links*. Direct links can be stronger or weaker depending on how close we are to the person and how much we communicate with them. The *strength of ties* refers to how strong or weak a direct link is. We can also be indirectly linked to people with whom we do not have a direct link. For example, I am *indirectly linked* to Dr. Shebib's family, whom I have yet to meet. The more people you would have to go through to be indirectly linked, the more *degrees of separation*.

Most of us have professional and personal networks. Our *professional networks* involve our work and occupation. Our *personal networks* involve friends and family. These can overlap. People also have joint and separate networks. For example, people whom both Dr. Shebib and I know are in our *joint network*. Joint networks are when there is *network overlap* or direct links in common. Separate networks, in contrast, are people directly linked to one person but not the other person. Professor Shebib and I both know Professor Boster, but she never met Jim McCroskey or Gerry Miller, just as I have not met some of her professors.

It is important to remember that networks are dynamic. They are always changing. People meet new people and make new connections. The links between people grow stronger or weaker. People can also disconnect from others. New links form, links get stronger or weaker, links drop, new people join, and other people leave the network. Networks can get larger, or they can shrink.

Centrality refers to a specific person's position within a network. The more interconnected someone is, the more central they are. These are people who seem to know everyone. The more direct and indirect links a person has and the stronger the ties, the more central the person is in the network. If we say that a person is well networked, that means that they are more central.

Opinion leaders are network members who are especially influential in their network. *Mavens* are people within a network who are seen by others as having some special knowledge or expertise. Opinion leaders tend to be centrally located within networks.

In contrast, people can be on the periphery of a network. Such people have few direct links and tend to be connected to people who also have few links. *Isolates* are people on the extreme periphery of networks and who are not well linked with others in a network. Note that an isolate in one network might be central in another. That person at work who keeps to themselves might have a tight circle of friends outside work or be deeply involved in their church.

Bridges are people who connect two different networks. *Gatekeepers* are people who control the flow of information within or between networks.

Density is a characteristic of networks. Dense networks are more interconnected. People within dense networks have lots of connections to others and fewer degrees of separation. Everyone knows everyone or at least knows someone who knows them. Small towns can be examples of dense networks. Collectivist cultures also tend to have denser networks.

Networks and Relationships

Networks, especially our social networks, can have a profound impact on our happiness, well-being, and quality of life. Way back in Chapter 1, we talked about the importance of social integration. Social integration means being enmeshed in a network with good, strong, direct ties to other people.

Networks have a way of perpetuating themselves. A common way we make new friends is through existing friends. Meeting people through other people is incredibly common. Sometimes it is intentional. People purposefully introduce people to others in their network. Other times, it is more coincidental. If I am spending time with someone, I am likely to have contact with the people they spend time with. As I mentioned, this can work for finding job opportunities. It is also one way people meet relational partners.

Once relationships are established, networks can affect relationships. Networks can be supportive of a relationship, or networks can interfere. For example, people in your network could decide that you and your romantic partner are not a good match. This happened to my brother. My parents, especially my mother, did not like my sister-in-law. My parents tried to break them up before marriage. As you can imagine, some serious conflict and hard feelings resulted.

There is a debunked finding from social psychology called the *Romeo and Juliet effect*.[1] The finding was that parental interference in romantic relationships tended to backfire and enhance the love in the targeted couple. Not only has the finding not been replicated, but more recent studies found the exact opposite.[2] One of my favorite communication studies found that having a more active and interconnected joint network and having a network that is supportive of your relationship is good for relational longevity.[3] In fact, if your friends and family really like your partner, it can be harder to break up. Fortunately, the more your friends and family like your partner, the more you like them too. Having a supportive network is one less source of stress and drama. That makes relationships easier.

Chapter Summary

- Networks map out who people communicate with.
- Networks are personally and professionally important.
- Important network concepts include degrees of separation, centrality, density, opinion leaders, and mavens.

Next up, in Chapter 22, Dr. Shebib reviews the role of personality in communication.

1. Driscoll et al. (1972).
2. Sinclair et al. (2014).
3. Parks and Adelman (1983).

Personality

[Dr. Levine's Voice]

In graduate school, Jim McCroskey (from Chapter 2) often called me a nerd. That did not bother me much because I was (and still am) secure, but I found it curious because that is not how I thought of myself. Looking back, however, he was right. It is interesting that he picked up on something about me that I had yet to realize about myself. He wrote a book on personality and communication.[1] Presumably, I had, without self-awareness, presented nerd-like qualities in my interactions with him, and he picked up on that.

In many ways, the people I am closest to are quite different from each other. Some, for example, are introverts; others are extroverts. They have diverse and wide-ranging interests. Some are big sports fans, others not at all. Some are foodies; others are not so much. But there is a pattern—a set of things they all have in common. They are all high on a personality trait called openness (see the following), and they all hold advanced degrees. My wife has a PhD. My good friend Steve also has a PhD, and so does his spouse. My friend Tom has two PhDs; his wife just has one. My friend Rene has a PhD and an MD, and his wife (also with a PhD) might be the smartest one in their family. My friends Dave and Kim also have PhDs. I like to spend time with smart, open-minded people, especially smart people who know about things I don't know much about. In terms of Chapter 12, I might be described as high in need of cognition. In the language of Professor James C. McCroskey, I am a nerd. My wife has a concept she calls ping-pong. Ping-pong is bouncing ideas back and forth, testing them out. I enjoy this sort of mental ping-pong. It is part of my personality, and it is expressed in my communication preferences and communication style. I have come to recognize that about myself and to embrace my status as a nerd.

Personality Traits

Personality is one type of *individual difference*. Individual differences are just what they sound like. They are ways in which people are different from other people. *Traits* are individual differences that hold (a) across situations and (b) over time. For example, my need for cognition is not just evident when talking with friends. I'm that way at work, when watching television, etc. I have also been that way for as long as I can remember. Traits can change over time, but they tend to be stable. Personality traits refer to stable tendencies people have that predispose them to respond in particular ways that differentiate them from the tendencies of other people. Traits can be affective, impacting how people feel; cognitive, reflecting how people think, and/or behavioral, involving what people tend to do.

*There is an important distinction between **traits** and **states**.* States exist here and now or at a point in time. If

---

1. McCroskey and Daly (1987).

we say that you are in a state of confusion, that means that you are confused at the moment. You could also be in a state of anxiety, a state of relaxation, or a state of bliss. States are, by definition, fleeting. We can think about moods, for example, in terms of states and traits. If I am in a good mood at this moment, that is a state. If I am an upbeat person who is usually in a good mood, that is a trait. Similarly, if we describe someone as moody, that is a trait description of someone who tends to have mood swings.

Personality is multifaceted and multidimensional. There are numerous personality dimensions. As mentioned in Chapter 15, dimensions are continual, along with people's differences. Differences in personality are typically expressed in gradations along various dimensions. In this chapter, I'll discuss several dimensions of personality that I find useful for understanding communication.

Intelligence

In my opening narrative, I referenced intelligence. Intelligence has an underappreciated role in communication and relationships. For example, it is one of the best predictors I know of mate selection. The correlation between spouses in IQ (a measure of general intelligence) is around .5.[2] That is quite a large effect.

Intelligence is not just book smarts. It is also different than being educated, although intelligence is a strong predictor of both academic performance and the highest degree a person will earn.

It is the mental ability to comprehend, plan, reason, think abstractly, problem solve, learn quickly, and so on. Intelligence impacts a variety of life outcomes, such as occupational choices, socioeconomic status, and how long people will live. Unfortunately, how it affects communication is not well studied. It determines, in part, what people like to talk about, the depth of those conversations, and who a person talks to. Communicating with someone who is too different from us in intelligence can be frustrating for both people.

The Big 5

The big five personality traits[3] are reflected in the acronym OCEAN. **Openness** (O) refers to people who are open-minded, like variety, are adventurous, are curious, creative, and have broad interests. C is **conscientiousness**; people who are organized, reliable, disciplined, scrupulous, and careful. **Extroversion** (E) is the extent to which a person is sociable, outgoing, and talkative. **Agreeableness** is about how good-natured, forgiving, and upbeat a person is. These are people we think of as being nice. Someone with a mean streak is low on agreeableness. Finally, N is the first letter in **neuroticism,** which involves trait anxiety. People high in neuroticism worry about things. People low in neuroticism are secure and chill.

Keep in mind that people can vary in each of these. You can be high on some, low on others, or anywhere in between. Also, keep in mind that like many other aspects of personality, there are at least three aspects to them. There is how we see ourselves, there is how we present ourselves, and then there is how someone else perceives us. These can converge or be quite different.

2. Lubinski (2004).
3. McCrae and Costa (1987).

The Dark Triad

Three socially disapproved dimensions of personality are Machiavellianism, psychopathy, and narcissism.[4] **Machiavellianism** refers to manipulative people. **Psychopathy** refers to people with high impulsivity, along with little empathy and low anxiety. Narcissism is discussed in the next section. While there is overlap between the three, they are arguably unique and distinguishable. For example, both Machiavellians and narcissists can be both charming and manipulative, but their motives are different. Machiavellians are more hedonistic; narcissists are motivated by boosting their own self-image. Both psychopathy and narcissism are characterized by a lack of empathy, but psychopathy is associated with more overtly antisocial behavior, whereas a narcissist is concerned with what other people think about them.

Narcissism

Narcissism gets special attention here because I think of it as the enemy of competent communication. Personality and clinical psychologists think about narcissism in a variety of ways. Here I focus on what might be called *compensatory narcissism*. This is when someone has low self-esteem and is deeply insecure, but they present themselves as just the opposite. Some characteristics of narcissism include grandiosity, a fragile self, a lack of empathy, the desire to be the center of attention, being manipulative, a sense of entitlement, and an inability to maintain lasting close relationships. In communication, they steer the topics of conversation back to themselves, they brag, they lie, they one-up others, and they are prone to extremely inappropriate self-disclosure.

Narcissism is especially detrimental to communication because communication is a mutual activity. Preoccupation with oneself and disregard for others works against competent communication. This said, they can be effective (especially in the short term) in manipulating others to feed their unquenchable ego needs. But for the people around them, this gets old over time. It gets exhausting. It is also a problem in the workplace because they do not take constructive feedback well, they hold grudges for perceived slights, and they do not care if others are treated fairly.

Some Communication Traits

Argumentativeness refers to people who like to argue and debate. **Verbal aggressiveness** describes people who insult and offend others. They say mean things. **Communication apprehension** involves people who experience anxiety when communicating, especially in public or when they are being evaluated. Communication apprehension is quite common in the general population but less so among communication majors. There is a disproportionately high number of extroverts in the academic field of communication.

Self and Observer Perspectives

A recurring theme in this chapter is that people's understanding of their own personalities does not always align with how others see them. With communication appreciation, for example, people tend to be very much aware of

---

4. Paulhus and Williams (2002).

their tendencies, especially after they have given a few speeches. However, many people are good at hiding their felt level of anxiety, so the audience cannot accurately assess what a speaker is feeling. Argumentative people tend to know they are argumentative, and so do others. Verbal aggressiveness is different. Some verbally aggressive people may not realize the extent to which they say hurtful things to others. Other people may think they are more verbally aggressive than they are. They like to imagine themselves as someone who would really tell someone off. But, when they are in that situation, they don't. Thus, the others that we interact with frequently know better than us how verbally aggressive we really are.

Some personality traits are quick and easy to spot. Extroverts, for example, are comparatively easy to spot, as is shyness. In my experience, it can take much longer and much more interaction to spot a narcissist.

Accurately assessing other people's personality traits is an important part of competent communication. The better able you are at noticing the tendencies of those you talk to, the better able you are to adapt your communication to them. For example, it might be wise to dial down any argumentative or verbally aggressive tendencies you might have when conversing with a more neurotic (to be considerate) or psychopathic (to avoid violence) person.

In my job as a department chair, it is good for me to know who is especially high in conscientiousness. I give those people important tasks that require attention to detail and that need to be done right. I do not assign them tasks that need to be done quickly or where quality is not paramount.

Knowing a person's personality can also aid in the targeting of persuasive messages. Conscientious people might be especially vulnerable to guilt nudges, and more neurotic people might be susceptible to fear appeals (not too much fear because you don't want to push a neurotic over the top). Social proof is not going to work on a Machiavellian or someone with a psychopathic personality.

A Communication Perspective[5]

In graduate school, I did an experiment demonstrating a communication perspective on personality. Most thinking about personality and communication follows one of two directions: either looking at how some personality trait predicts how someone will communicate or looking at how some personality trait predicts how someone will respond to some type of communication. I thought, and I still do, that we need to integrate sender and receiver personalities. How a conversation between two people goes depends not just on the personalities of each person but on the interplay of the personalities. Some personalities play well together, others clash. Some personality traits overwhelm or facilitate others.

Chapter Summary

- *Personality traits* are stable tendencies people have that predispose people to respond in particular ways.
- *Traits* can be distinguished from *states*. States are fleeting; traits are more stable.
- The big five personality traits are (O) openness, (C), conscientiousness, (E) extroversion, (A) agreeableness, and (N) neuroticism.
- The dark triad includes Machiavellianism, psychopathy, and narcissism.

5. Levine and Boster (1996).

- Narcissism is harmful to competent communication.
- Three communication personality traits include argumentativeness, verbal aggressiveness, and communication appreciation.
- Understanding others' personalities is useful in adapting our communication to who we are talking to.

Next up, Dr. Shebib will discuss family communication.

CHAPTER 23

Family Communication

[*Dr. Shebib's Voice*]

L et me begin this chapter by giving you some background on myself and my family. I am 50% Dutch and 50% Lebanese. My paternal great grandparents immigrated from Beirut, Lebanon, to escape persecution by the Turkish government. They fled their country to escape the violence and repression that they were experiencing in Lebanon and came to the United States to live the American dream. My maternal grandparents immigrated from Amsterdam, Holland. My maternal grandfather, my Opa, a retired professor of emeritus in psychology at the State University of New York, was 10 years old on May 10, 1940, when the Nazis invaded Holland. His brother is a Holocaust survivor who was forced into a concentration camp for nearly 5 years because he was *too educated*. My Opa would commute by bike weekly to check on the status of his brother. One day during his weekly bike ride in November of 1944, a noncombatant civilian, my Opa, was mowed down by a German soldier, who decided to fire several rounds of his machine gun on innocent civilians, one of which was him. An American Medical Corps man found him unconscious and took him to their hospital, where he was treated for multiple machine gun bullets and phosphoric tracer bullets in his upper right thigh. Decades later, when choosing to start his family, my Opa decided he could not raise his children in a place that was once an occupied territory—in a place where once his parents couldn't protect him. Both my maternal and paternal grandparents left their home country to give their children a better life here in the United States.

The horrible experiences that both sets of my grandparents faced have affected absolute changes in my life. Their stories made me aware of the potential range and/or intensity that interpersonal violence or group conflict can provoke. It may surprise you to learn that the most important part of me that changed when I was given the information of my grandparents' stories was my firm belief that war, all wars, constitute a regression of the human spirit to its most base level of depravity. And that those who start wars, no matter the cause (religion, land, power), commit crimes against humanity. Thus, the essence is that families shape you, which subsequently influences your opinions, beliefs, attitudes, and subsequently your behavior and communication.

I would like to dedicate this chapter to my Opa, Dr. Arthur Cryns, who passed away while I was writing this chapter on January 25, 2023.

Defining Family

When I say the word "family," who is the first person you think of? How would you define families? Who can be included in your family, and who can't be included in your family? At first glimpse, this may seem to be an easy question, but when you intuitively think about it, it is much more complex.

Family relationships are some of the most important and long-lasting ones we will have in our entire lives. Although other disciplines study family relationships, communication scholars focus on the power of communication within families. Indeed, how we create a family, maintain family relationships, and even distance ourselves from family members requires communication. But before we get into this discussion, we need to define family. Traditionally, family communication scholars define family in one of three ways.

The first way to define family is *structurally* based on form. Structural definitions rely on specific criteria (e.g., blood ties, law) to determine family membership. The second way to define family is *functionally* based on the task. Functional definitions view family as at least one adult and one or more other persons who perform certain tasks of the family life, such as nurturance, socialization, development, and financial and emotional support. Functional definitions offer more flexibility than structural definitions but still tend to highlight reproduction and child-rearing. Finally, the third way to define family is *transactionally* based on interaction. A transactional definition emphasizes the communication among family members and the subjective feelings generated by an interaction. This emphasizes the role communication plays in constituting what it means to be a family. Relationships, then, are familial to the extent that members feel and act like a family.

Attachment Theory

Attachment refers to an emotional bond forged between an infant and the primary caregiver. Bowlby[1] postulated that the initial bonds established by children with their caregivers exert a profound and enduring influence on their lives. At the core of attachment theory lies the principle that primary caregivers, when accessible and responsive to an infant's needs, foster the development of a profound sense of security. This process enables the infant to understand that the caregiver can be relied upon, establishing a secure foundation from which the child can confidently explore the world.

Attachment theorists posit that individuals possess diverse attachment styles based on their self-perception and perception of others. These perceptions, known as *internal working models*, serve as cognitive representations of oneself and potential partners, shaped by past experiences in close relationships, with the infant-caregiver being the most significant relationship influencing internal working models. These models aid individuals in comprehending the complexities of the world around them.[2] The model of self falls along a positive-negative continuum, as does the model of others.

Early communication with primary caregivers plays a pivotal role in shaping a child's internal working model of themselves and others, thereby establishing a foundation for future attachments.[3] The initial 2 to 3 years of life, with particular emphasis on the first year, are crucial for the formation of these internal models. Even as early as 6 weeks old, infants exhibit a natural inclination toward their primary caregiver, typically the mother.

An infamous longitudinal study in Baltimore referred to as the "strange situation"[4] was designed to look at the relationship between attachment and infants' exploration of their surroundings. The researchers carried out a controlled observation by documenting the responses of a child and their mother (caregiver) in an unfamiliar room filled with toys. Approximately 100 infants and their mothers from middle-class American backgrounds took part in the strange situation study. The purpose of the strange situation procedure was to create an environment that was new enough to encourage exploratory behavior in the child yet not so unfamiliar as to provoke fear or intensify attachment-related behaviors from the beginning. The room was arranged with a clearly defined 9

1. Bowlby (1982).

2. Bowlby (1973), Bretherton and Munholland (2008), and Collins and Read (1994).

3. Ainsworth et al. (1978) and Bowlby (1977).

4. Ainsworth et al. (1971).

× 9-foot floor space divided into 16 squares, allowing for the recording of the child's location and movements. On one end of the room, there was a chair adorned with toys, while the other end had chairs for the mother and a stranger. The baby was positioned in the center, free to move about. The mother and stranger were given instructions in advance regarding their respective roles. The researchers observed from the other side of a one-way mirror, so the children did not know they were being observed.

Essentially, the researchers were interested to see how the child reacts when the primary caregiver leaves the room and returns. This study led to the development of three types of attachment styles in infancy: (1) secure, (2) avoidant, and (3) anxious-ambivalent.[5]

Secure attached children explored the new environment and were moderately distressed when the caregiver left the room. Secure children tend to have responsive and warm parents, to receive moderate levels of stimulation, and to engage in synchronized interaction with their caregivers. Children who develop secure attachments to a caregiver are more likely to feel free to explore, approach others, and be positive toward strangers than are insecure types. Secure children are also likely to protest separation and then to show happiness when reunited with their caregivers. These children tend to develop positive models of self and others.

Avoidant attached children tend to have caregivers who are either insensitive to their signals or try too hard to please. In addition, avoidant children are often either over- or understimulated, which leads to physiological arousal and a flight response. When overstimulated, they retreat from social interaction to avoid being overloaded. When understimulated, they learn how to cope without social interaction. Because their caregivers are not able to fulfill their needs, they develop negative models of others. These children stay within themselves, seldom explore their environment, and are rarely positive toward strangers. They tend not to protest separation from caregivers and show little emotion when the caregiver returns.

Anxious-ambivalent attached children tend to be the product of inconsistent caregiver communication; sometimes the caregiver is appropriately responsive, and other times, the caregiver is neglectful or overstimulating. Anxious-ambivalent children often have caregivers who are preoccupied with their own problems, such as relational conflict, divorce, or substance abuse. Instead of blaming the caregiver (or the caregiver's situation) for this inconsistency, they blame themselves and develop self-models of doubt, insecurity, and uncertainty. Anxious-ambivalent children often are tentative when exploring their environment in the presence of their caregivers and fearful of exploration if alone. They protest separation from caregivers vehemently yet are both relieved and angry when the caregiver returns. This contradiction is reflected in their label—they are anxious upon separation and ambivalent when the caregiver returns. Sometimes these children develop positive models of others because they do receive some comfort and security from caregivers.

Family Communication Patterns (FCP)

FCP[6] was developed based on work from the cognitive theory of coorientation,[7] which was interested in how families need to develop a shared reality, which they do through communication. The communication strategies that people exhibit depend heavily on how they were socialized by their family to behave and communicate (or *not*). Communication patterns in families refer to repeated interaction styles and behaviors. A single family

5. Ainsworth (1969, 1982, 1989), Ainsworth et al. (1978), Ainsworth and Eichberg (1991), and Ainsworth and Wittig (1969).
6. Ritchie and Fitzpatrick (1990).
7. Heider (1946, 1958) and Newcomb (1953).

member's communication behavior over time can be patterned, but family communication scholars tend to focus on patterns among family members.

Family relationships are typically involuntary and long-lasting. One usually cannot choose one's siblings, for instance, and sibling relationships—even strained ones—commonly endure for most of one's lifetime. The involuntary and lengthy nature of family relations provides myriad opportunities for various communication patterns to emerge. The meaning of any particular interaction between family members is informed by previously established communication patterns, sometimes even patterns involving previous generations. Such FCPs are so central to family life that some scholars state that the very nature of family relationships is constituted by the ongoing pattern of exchanges. FCP consists of two orientations: conformity and conversation orientation. These two fundamental dimensions differentiate how families communicate and have been related to a variety of functional and dysfunctional familial consequences.[8]

The first fundamental dimension of FCP is conformity orientation. **Conformity orientation** is the degree to which a family fosters a climate where parents are the authority figures, and there is a strict adherence to family rules and norms. The family stresses uniformity and homogeneity of ideas, beliefs, attitudes, and opinions.[9] Thus, families high on the conformity orientation dimension have interactions characterized by children's strict obedience to parents, as well as "harmony, conflict avoidance, and the interdependence of family members."[10] Families low on the conformity orientation dimension have interactions characterized by the individuality of family members.

The second fundamental dimension of FCP is conversation orientation. **Conversation orientation** is the degree to which a family fosters open communication between one another. Therefore, the family stresses diversity and heterogeneity of ideas, beliefs, attitudes, and opinions. A highly conversation-oriented family values the uniqueness and individuality of family members and spur-of-the-moment and unconfined interactions. Families low in the conversation orientation dimension interact less frequently with one another, with few topics openly discussed between the family members.[11]

Family Types

Conversation and conformity orientations are not discrete categories but rather continuous dimensions,[12] and they crisscross to create a theoretical space that distinguishes four types of families.[13]

The first family type is the **pluralistic family**. Pluralistic families are high in conversation orientation while low in conformity orientation.[14] They make decisions as a family unit by openly discussing a variety of topics and valuing the individuality of each member of the family. Children in pluralistic families value family conversations,

8. Fitzpatrick and Ritchie (1994) and Koerner and Fitzpatrick (2002a).
9. Koerner and Fitzpatrick (2002a).
10. Koerner and Fitzpatrick (2002a, p. 86).
11. Koerner and Fitzpatrick (2002a).
12. Koerner and Schrodt (2014).
13. Ledbetter (2019).
14. Koerner and Fitzpatrick (2002b).

while at the same time learning to be independent and autonomous.[15] Briefly put, pluralistic families have open and frequent communication, and decisions are made together as a family.

The second type of family is the **consensual family**. Consensual families are high in both conversation and conformity orientations. In these families, parents make the decisions, but they also encourage open communication. Children in consensual families prioritize family conversations and tend to embrace their parents' beliefs and values.[16] Briefly put, consensual families have open and frequent communication but believe parents alone are the decision makers.

The third family type is the **protective family**. Protective families are low in conversation orientation while high in conformity orientation. These families often depend on the parents to make decisions, emphasize compliance with authority, and similarity of beliefs and values. Additionally, they only discuss a few topics openly in the family relationship. Children in protective families discover that there is little value in family conversations and that they should doubt their own decision-making skills.[17] Briefly put, protective families expect children to follow the parents' rules without questioning their authority.

Lastly, **laissez-faire families** are low in both conversation and conformity orientations. They do not spend a lot of time with one another, and when they do, they do not openly discuss a wide variety of topics.[18] Children in laissez-faire families learn to independently make their own decisions and believe there is little value in family conversations.[19] Briefly put, laissez-faire families don't value open and frequent communication, parental authority, or hierarchy. Kids can make decisions without much parental involvement.

Chapter Summary

- Defining families is complex.
- In childhood, the need to develop attachments is an innate and necessary part of human development.
- Attachment theory takes a social-developmental approach, stressing how interactions with others affect people's attachment style across the life span.

Next up, I will discuss my specialty, conflict!

---

15. Koerner and Fitzpatrick (2006a, 2006b).
16. Koerner and Fitzpatrick (2002b).
17. Koerner and Fitzpatrick (2006a, 2006b).
18. Koerner and Fitzpatrick (2002b).
19. Koerner and Fitzpatrick (2006a, 2006b).

CHAPTER 24

Conflict

[Dr. Shebib's Voice]

There's a scene in the movie *The Breakup*, which stars Jennifer Aniston and Vince Vaughan, highlights how conflict escalation can occur so perfectly. Jennifer Aniston, who plays Brooke, is cohabitating with Vince Vaughan's character, Gary. After arriving home from a long day, Brooke comes home to Gary on the couch playing video games. Brooke says, "Well, I'm going to do the dishes," as Gary responds, "Cool." Brooke, who is now annoyed, rolls her eyes, and says, "It would be nice if you'd help me." Gary completely ignores her, saying, "Damn it," referring to his video game. The conflict quickly spirals and escalates within a matter of minutes. Asking for help to do the dishes turns into 90 million (being sarcastic here) other problems in their relationship. To me, this scene is a textbook example (pun intended) of the escalation of dysfunctional conflict communication. If you'd like to watch the clip, check it out below!

My master's thesis, my doctoral preliminary study, and my doctoral dissertation are all about conflict. Explaining my interest in the topic involves some personal disclosure. My parents are literally my best friends, but growing up, my parents engaged in a lot of dysfunctional and destructive conflict behaviors with each other. At one point in my life, my parents were separated, not legally separated, as there isn't such a thing in the state of Michigan. It really had a big impact on me. It's literally what I do for a living—I study conflict. In terms of my scholarship on conflict, my overall research question is how to change dysfunctional conflict to functional once it becomes such a habit in a relationship.

Conflict is inevitable. We can't escape it—we can try to avoid it, but it will come about at some point, especially in our close relationships. Additionally, conflict has its utility, too. So, it's something we're going to have to learn to do properly, constructively, and functionally. And something I find so interesting about conflict is the intergenerational transmission of conflict communication. That is, children first learn about conflict from their parents (or caregivers). From a young age, we view our parents (or caregivers) as engaging (or not) in conflict. Thus, we are socialized[1] to handle conflict in ways like our observations of our family of origin. And therefore,

---

1. Koerner and Fitzpatrick (2002a, 2002b), Reese-Weber and Bartle-Haring (1998), and Shebib et al. (2020).

we pass down communication skills during conflict to our children, and if it's dysfunctional, they are more likely to handle conflict dysfunctionally in their future and subsequent interpersonal relationships. But this can also be extremely beneficial—if we handle conflict in collaborative and compromising ways, then we teach children these functional conflict behaviors. Throughout this chapter, I will highlight both the benefits of conflict and the destructive patterns that need to dissipate for the success and longevity of your close relationships!

What Is Conflict?

Conflict often carries a bad reputation because it is typically associated with a negative connotation. When people think about conflict, they typically relate conflict with dysfunctional communication behaviors, like yelling, arguing, and relational problems. However, conflict does not have to be an unhealthy event in your relationship. There are many benefits that can emerge from engaging in conflict. Nevertheless, what makes the most difference regarding conflict being beneficial or destructive in your relationship all depends on communication (both verbal and nonverbal). **Conflict** is defined as "an expressed struggle between at least two interdependent parties who perceive incompatible goals, scarce resources, and interference from others in achieving their goals."[2]

Some psychologists believe that humans are ruled by two connected contradictory mental structures, which they refer to as the hot system and the cool system. The hot system, which is located in the part of the brain called the amygdala, is emotional and fast. It is triggered whenever we feel a threat or some type of danger, which results in automatic fight-or-flight tendencies. The cool system, which is associated with the prefrontal cortex, is rational and slow. It encourages us to stop and think. Conflict is something that people find to be stressful, and we know that stress undermines our ability to rationalize. When we are under stress, we have tendencies to say and do things that result in triggering reactive emotions from other people.

Conflict Patterns

Negative Reciprocity

Even though we know that yelling and fighting have negative and destructive effects on relationships, people use these strategies quite often.[3] This may be because of the principle of *negative reciprocity*, a pattern whereby aggression precipitates more aggression. Once one person uses negativity or hostile remarks, the other person is likely to follow suit.[4]

There are two other tactics that have a tendency to escalate negativity during conflict. The first tactic is called *gunnysacking*. Gunnysacking[5] occurs when people store up their grievances and dump them on their partner during a conflict episode. "Rather than discussing each issue when it first surfaces, issues are placed in a metaphorical gunnysack and presented all at once." The second tactic is *kitchen sinking*. Kitchen sinking[6] occurs

2. Hocker and Wilmot (2013, p. 13).

3. Canary et al. (1995) and Sillars (1980).

4. Alberts (1988) and Gottman (1994).

5. Bach and Wyden (1970).

6. Bach and Wyden (1970).

when people rehash their old arguments when they get into a new one. Because gunnysacking and kitchen sinking involve attacking your partner, partners are likely to feel defensive and overwhelmed, making it difficult to discuss any of the issues productively.

Regardless of what specific behaviors couples use, those who engage in patterns of negative reciprocity report less relational satisfaction.[7] The key is to assess the ratio of positive and negative behaviors communicated during conflict. Research demonstrates that happy couples tend to engage in about five positive behaviors for every negative behavior, whereas the ratio of negative-to-positive behaviors was about one to one for unhappy couples.[8]

Demand-Withdraw

The demand-withdraw pattern is a commonly reoccurring and dysfunctional conflict sequence where one partner makes demands on the other person (by complaining or criticizing), while the other partner withdraws from the interaction with defensiveness or passive inaction.[9]

The person in the demanding position is likely to be in a less powerful position (relative to the partner) and tends to be dissatisfied with something. By contrast, the person in the withdrawing position is likely to be in a more powerful position and to be happy with the status quo. This pattern is commonly found in marriages where the wife is more likely to be the demander, and the husband is more likely to withdraw. Couples who use the demand-withdrawal pattern may have problems with punctuation, with each partner "punctuating" the cause of the conflict differently. One partner might say, "I have to nag you all the time because you always withdraw," whereas the other partner might say, "I have to withdraw because you are always nagging me." Notice that both partners blame the other for their behavior.

The Four Horsemen of the Apocalypse

Many couples find it difficult to accept that it is not the presence of conflict that indicates a troubled relationship. Conflict is inevitable and a normal and even healthy part of a relationship. It's how you deal with conflict that can potentially be problematic.

Research has shown there are certain kinds of negative communication styles that are so destructive, that they signal the demise of a relationship. A relationship expert and best-selling author, Dr. John Gottman, calls these the four horsemen of the apocalypse, a metaphor used to describe counterproductive behaviors that are so lethal they predict relationship failure if they aren't changed. The metaphor depicts the end of times in the New Testament. They describe conquest, war, hunger, and death, respectively. We use this metaphor to describe communication styles that, according to research, can predict the demise and end of a relationship. This is because each of the four horsemen corrodes the love that is at the core of an intimate relationship.

According to Gottman, couples who divorce are likely to exhibit a conflict pattern that includes the following four types of communication: (1) criticism, (2) defensiveness, (3) contempt, and (4) stonewalling, with contempt and stonewalling particularly toxic to relationships. Gottman's research suggests that within the first

---

7. Canary et al. (1995) and Sillars (1980).

8. Gottman (1994).

9. Christensen and Heavey (1990).

three minutes of an interaction, the presence of these forms of communication can predict divorce with an accuracy rate of over 92%.[10]

Criticisms

Criticism refers to attacking or putting down your partner's personality or character rather than his or her behavior itself. When you criticize your partner, you are basically implying that there is something wrong with him or her. There's a big difference between a complaint and a criticism. Criticisms can revolve around personal characteristics, including negative remarks about personality, appearance, or performance. Criticisms are problematic because they focus on blaming the partner, which can cause an escalation of conflict.

A complaint addresses a specific action or nonaction and is different from criticism in that a complaint targets a behavior you want to change. Therefore, complaints focus on a specific behavior. Researchers have noted that often complaints are healthy. If relational partners never complained, they would be unable to improve their relationships by changing problematic behavior. Therefore, an *antidote for criticism* is a behavioral complaint. Other antidotes to criticisms involve talking about your feelings using "I" statements and expressing a positive need.[11]

Defensiveness

The second horseman is defensiveness, and it is usually a response to criticisms. People use defensive tactics when they feel this need to protect themselves. One defensive behavior that has been researched immensely is *mind reading*. Mind reading occurs when people assume that they know their partner's feelings, motives, and behaviors. Imagine someone saying to you, "You never care how I feel, and you always get tense in situations like this." However, this is not true. Your partner would be assuming you do not care and that you get tense instead of listening and verifying how you really feel. Because your partner's guesses are wrong, defensiveness is likely to ensue, and you are likely to be frustrated and even offended that your partner could misinterpret you so much. Mind-reading statements often include the words "you always" or "you never." Thus, the *antidote for defensiveness* is to fight the impulse to defend oneself and instead accept at least partial responsibility.[12]

Contempt

The third horseman is contempt, and it's my favorite, probably because it's the most lethal and "darker" than the rest. Contempt goes far beyond criticism. While criticism attacks your partner's character, contempt assumes a position of moral superiority over them (e.g., "You're crazy").

When we communicate in this state, we are truly mean—we treat others with disrespect, mock them with sarcasm, ridicule, call them names, or mimic or use body language such as eye-rolling or sneering. Contempt is fueled by long-simmering negative thoughts about one's partner, and it arises in the form of an attack on someone's sense of self. In other words, these are comments that belittle or demean the other person. It's virtually

10. Gottman (1994).
11. Gottman Institute (2023).
12. Gottman Institute (2023).

impossible to resolve a problem when your partner is getting the message that you're disgusted with them and that you're condescending and acting as their superior.

Research[13] has found that couples who are contemptuous of each other are more likely to suffer from infectious illnesses (colds, the flu, etc.) than couples who are not contemptuous due to their weakened immune system. Let me reiterate this: contempt erodes your partner's immune system. That is, my being contemptuous of my partner has a negative effect on their immune system. That is crazy, but it's because contempt is the most poisonous of all relationship killers.

I cannot emphasize that enough. Contempt destroys psychological, emotional, and physical health. The *antidote for contempt* is to start small and describe your feelings; avoid "you" statements. Build a culture of appreciation by reminding yourself of your partner's positive qualities and find gratitude for positive actions.[14]

Stonewalling

The fourth horseman is stonewalling, which occurs when the listener withdraws from the interaction, shuts down, and simply stops responding to their partner. Rather than confronting the issues with their partner, people who stonewall can make evasive maneuvers, such as tuning out, turning away, acting busy, or engaging in obsessive or distracting behaviors. Partners are no longer trying to work problems out and instead avoid each other and generally separate from each other.

It takes time for the negativity created by the first three horsemen to become overwhelming enough that stonewalling becomes an understandable "out," but when it does, it frequently becomes a bad habit. And unfortunately, stonewalling isn't easy to stop. It is a result of feeling physiologically flooded, and when we stonewall, we may not even be in a psychological state where we can discuss things rationally. Thus, the *antidote for stonewalling*[15] is physiological self-soothing by taking a break from the conflict to cool down and let the negativity dissipate before discussing it in more detail.

Chapter Summary

- Conflict is *not* always bad.
- Communication is key.
- Use the antidotes!
- Even if you have good intentions and know how you should act during a conflict situation, when your emotions are running high, it is difficult not to violate some of these rules.
- If you find yourself engaging in some destructive tactics during conflict situations, do not panic—even experts in conflict, like myself, make mistakes.
- Recognizing these mistakes is a first step toward managing conflict in ways that keep your relationships satisfying.

13. Kiecolt-Glaser and Newton (2001).
14. Gottman Institute (2023).
15. Gottman Institute (2023).

In the next chapter, Dr. Levine will discuss what he is best known for—deception (I like to refer to him as the Godfather of Deception)!

CHAPTER 25

Deception

[Dr. Levine's Voice]

Early in my career, I coauthored a series of influential studies on deception with Steve McCornack. This early work brought us into contact with some of the leading deception theorists-researchers of the time. In the early 1990s, when this opening story took place, deception research was beginning to fracture. Disagreements over theory, research designs, and the interpretation of findings were building into vitriolic academic feuds. Two of the most accomplished professors back then had a particularly acrimonious falling out. While some of this conflict was published in a back-and-forth series of articles, that was just the tip of the iceberg. I know this because one of the famous professors was forwarding me the email correspondence between the two. Sometime later, I was talking with the second famous professor who told me their version of events. The version they told me presented themselves in a much more favorable light and portrayed the other professor much less favorably than the emails I had read. I knew what I was being told was false, and I surmised that I was being lied to. To this day, one of those professors is on my do-not-trust list. Since then, I have discovered many more reasons to distrust that person.

More recently, in my current role as department chair, I was sitting in my office one morning, and a student came in to make a complaint. The student said that their professor had pornography briefly up on the screen in class. The student did not think it was intentional and said that the professor got it down as quickly as possible, but the student found it upsetting and unprofessional. They believed that this should not have happened and felt an obligation to report the incident. I thanked them and told them that I would investigate. I talked with the professor. The professor categorically denied the incident and suggested that the student was the type of person who might imagine such things or make false accusations. The professor assured me that the student's version of events did not happen. Almost certainly, one of them was lying.

Before continuing the story, I have three questions for you. First, who should I believe? Why? Third, what do you think happened next?

Two things happened next. First, other students in the class were interviewed and asked if anything out of the ordinary happened in class on that day. Second, since the professor was using a university laptop, the laptop was confiscated for forensic analysis. Several other students corroborated the first student's version of events. Everyone who was paying attention saw it and independently provided similar accounts. Second, there was porn on the laptop. After learning this additional information, I was confident that I knew who was lying, and I had an accurate understanding of what took place.

Defining Deception

I define **deception** as *intentionally, knowingly, or functionally misleading another person*. This definition excludes honest mistakes. It also excludes transparent falsehoods that are not meant to be misleading, like sarcasm. A true statement, however, can be deceptive if it is misleading and leads another person to a false conclusion.

In deciding to label an instance of communication as deceptive, I consider four questions. Did what was communicated or implied differ in an important way from the truth? Did the sender know, or should they have known, that the message was false or misleading? Would a reasonable member of the language community be misled by the message? Finally, did the misleading nature of the message serve a function of hiding the truth and/or presenting an alternative account that worked in the communicator's interest in a way that the truth did not? If the answer to all four questions is yes, then the communication is deceptive.

Four Ways to Deceive With Words

The work of Steve McCornack suggests that there are four ways to verbally deceive others.[1] First and most obviously, people can say things that are false and knowingly communicate the false information as if it were true. This is what we usually think of as an outright **lie** and is what Steve calls **bald-face lies**. More typically, people just weave a bit of false information into an otherwise truthful statement.

The second way people deceive others is through **omission**. This is by far the most common type of deception because it is the easiest. If you do not want someone to know something, you can just not mention it.

The last two methods are **equivocation** and **evasion**. Being equivocal leaves open multiple interpretations, and what is meant is unclear, and thus the truth is obscured. Evasion involves actively steering a conversion away from the hidden information.

We can also distinguish between **blunt honesty** (bald-faced truth) and **packaged truths**.[2] Bluntness involves saying things without regard for how they will be heard by others and risks being hurtful or considered rude. Packaged truths are not meant to be deceptive so much as to be honest while also being polite and considerate. Honest communication is often shaded and padded to be palatable and socially appropriate. I do not think of this packaging as deceptive. That is not the point of it.

Research Findings

Research finds that most people believe that nonverbal **cues** signal lying. Cues are specific behaviors that function as "tells." The most common folk belief about lying is that liars will not look you in the eye. That is, they avert their gaze. Many people also believe that liars appear nervous or lack confidence and conviction.[3]

Interestingly, even though the belief that liars avert their gaze is held worldwide, it has no validity. Honest speakers and liars do not differ in eye behavior. They do look down or this way or that way. Cues have much less utility than people think. Even the most useful cues only have value probabilistically over large numbers of people.

---

1. McCornack (1992).
2. McCornack (1997).
3. Bond and The Global Research Team (2006).

They cannot be used to tell that some person is lying in some instance in a way that holds up across people and situations.[4]

People also overestimate their ability to detect lies. Most people think they can tell when someone is lying, but experiments find that people are just 54% accurate at distinguishing truths from lies.[5] Research also finds that people are **truth-biased**. People are more likely to believe people than not. There are ways to detect lies, but as the stories at the beginning of the chapter illustrated, effective methods of lie detection are not based on behavior observation or on reading nonverbal communication.

Truth-Default Theory

All the stories that begin the various chapters in this book are true and honest. You probably never considered that they might not be until you read this. If this is the case, it is an example of the truth-default.

I created *truth-default theory* and wrote a book about it.[6] The basic idea is that honesty is the default mode of communication. People are honest unless they have a reason not to be. That is, deception requires a motive. Motives for deception happen when the goals of the communication do not align with the truth. Even then, some people will be honest. But, when the truth works fine for people, they are almost invariably honest.

Truth-default theory predicts that most people are honest most of the time and that deception is infrequent relative to honest communication. Further, most people are more honest than average, and most lies are told by a *few prolific liars*. That is, the frequency of lying is skewed. The small percentage of people who lie often inflate the average. On any given day, most people tell between zero and two lies.

People who lie prolifically are not necessarily dishonest people, although they might be. Some people, for example, might have jobs that require telling a particular lie over and over, and they do not lie much otherwise.

The other side of defaulting to the truth is that we tend to believe other people. Often, the thought that someone might be deceiving us does not come to mind. According to truth-default theory, suspecting deception and deciding that a certain communication is deceptive requires *triggers*. For example, in my opening story, the trigger was that I was being told information that contradicted my prior knowledge. In the second story, the discrepancies between the student's and the professor's versions of the events triggered suspicion. I knew someone was lying. The results of the investigation (evidence) triggered me to judge that the professor's denial was a lie and that the student was honest.

The tendency to passively believe others (defaulting to the truth) makes us vulnerable to deception. Sometimes we get duped. According to truth-default theory, although getting deceived can be traumatic and harmful, there is a huge upside to believing others. We need to default to the truth to communicate efficiently. Communication lets us learn from others. It allows us to cooperate, work together, and coordinate our activities with others. It allows us to get to know other people, make connections, and establish communities and relationships. None of these valuable outcomes are served by distrusting people and second-guessing everything we hear. Without the truth-default, we would be bogged down in uncertainty and isolated by our distrust.

Truth-default theory distinguishes between cues, demeanor, and content. *Cues* are specific behaviors like a smile, eye blink, the direction of gaze, or a hand movement. *Demeanor* is the overall impression a person gives

---

4. DePaulo et al. (2003).
5. Bond and DePaulo (2006).
6. Levine (2020).

off. People, for example, can come off as friendly or nervous. Demeanor is conveyed by combinations of cues. For example, friendliness is conveyed not just by smiling but also by tone of voice, touch, body orientation, etc. One of the insights offered by truth-default theory is that cues do not travel alone but work together to create a demeanor. Demeanor is much more impactful than specific cues, and it determines how likely we are to believe someone. We are more likely to believe people who come off as friendly, confident extroverts. We are less likely to believe people with anxious or socially awkward demeanors. This is a big part of the reason people do poorly in deception detection experiments. A person's demeanor is not diagnostic of their honesty.

Content involves the meaning of words and what is being said. According to truth-default theory, carefully listening to what is said, understanding what is said in context, and applying critical thinking (and evidence if possible) is a better way to not be deceived. Think back to the two stories at the beginning of the chapter. See how the lies were detected? Both examples involved communication content, not cues or demeanor. Also, notice that the lie in the second story was detected well after the fact. According to truth-default theory, many lies are only detected later.

The Limits of 54%

The major finding of deception detection experiments is that people are only slightly better than chance at distinguishing truths from lies. The average accuracy is just 54%. Truth-default theory contextualizes this finding telling us when it does and does not apply. First up, 54% applies to prompted deception detection tasks. That is, people in deception detection experiments are asked if some communication is deceptive or not. People are triggered as part of the experiment. Of course, in everyday communication, we are not prompted to consider deception. According to truth-default theory, if there is no prompt or trigger, people will just believe. If the communication is deceptive, they are fooled.

This leads us to the idea of the *veracity effect*. Because people default to the truth or are truth-biased, they correctly believe honest communication and incorrectly believe false and misleading communication. That is, people get truths right and lies wrong. The word veracity means the truth or falsity of something. The veracity effect is that if you are right or wrong in believing something depends on the truth or falsity of the communication. The more likely the communication is to be honest, the more accurate people are.

Deception detection experiments producing 54% accuracy expose people to an equal number of truths and lies. Because of the veracity effect, if communication is more than 50–50 likely to be honest, then accuracy would be better. However, accuracy would be even worse if most communication was dishonest. But most communication is honest.

Finally, according to Truth-default theory (TDT), there are five ways to do better than 54%. The best thing is to use evidence and fact-check what is said if possible. Besides fact-checking, listen for content and be sure to understand content in its context. This can make plausibility helpful. Does what is said sound reasonable? Because people lie for a reason, paying attention to a person's motives is useful. You can ask questions to try to get information that can be fact-checked or that is relevant to plausibility and motive. Finally, sometimes you can persuade people to be honest with you.

Here is how I approach detecting deception in my daily life. First up, I ask myself if the topic or issue is important to me. Does it matter much? If not, I don't worry about it and just give people the benefit of the doubt. If it is important, I try to have as much background knowledge as possible. Sometimes I will do some research up front and ask questions where I already know the answer. Otherwise, I will remember what was said and fact-check as much as possible. I ask myself, does what was said make sense? How likely is it? Do they have a motive to deceive me? If it is plausible and there is no motive, I lower my guard a bit. If I am suspicious, I will ask questions and try to get the person to be honest with me.

At the end of the day, I don't worry much about deception. If it is something important, the truth may come out at some point. If someone deceives me about something important, then I learn not to trust them, and I warn others about their lack of trustworthiness. Chronic suspicion is unhealthy.

Chapter Summary

- Deception is intentionally, knowingly, or functionally misleading another person.
- Deception can involve conveying false information, omission, equivocation, or evasion.
- Nonverbal cues like avoiding eye contact are not useful in lie detection.
- Honesty is the default mode of communication. People are usually honest unless they have a motive to lie, and people believe other people unless they have a reason not to.
- Most communication is honest, but there are a few prolific liars.
- Improving lie detection involves carefully listening to communication content and understanding what is in context.
- Most lies are detected after the fact by using evidence.

The final chapter is up next. It covers being a good communicator. Really, this whole book has been about being a good communicator, so I will try to tie things together.

CHAPTER 26

Communication Competence

[Dr. Levine's voice]

I attended my first communication conference as an undergraduate student. It was the annual meeting of the Western Communication Association in Fresno, California. That is where I first met Jim McCroskey and Michael Beatty, who recruited me to graduate school. While there, I attended a panel in which four speakers presented their research, followed by a respondent who provided commentary. One of the presenters was a graduate student who was visibly (and understandably) nervous. The respondent, an older professor, eviscerated the student on his presentation style. It was brutal. The basic message was that this was a communication conference, we expect better, you embarrassed yourself and your university, and you do not belong here. To me, the irony was as striking as the brutality. Fortunately, I have since learned that that was an isolated incident and very much atypical. This leads to my first bit of advice about communication. Don't be a jerk.

Being a good communicator is part of what it means to be educated. Of course, not every educated person communicates competently. But, if you ask people about the skill sets, competencies, and knowledge bases of a well-educated person, communication is always high on this list, along with critical thinking, writing skills, quantitative literacy, scientific reasoning, a knowledge of history, and an appreciation of the humanities, etc. As mentioned in the first chapter, communication skills are highly valued by employers. Communication skills also facilitate social integration, which is good for our health and well-being.

One of the challenging things about being a communication professor (or a communication major) is that many people do not understand what that entails or what the field of communication is about. My parents never really understood. Communication, as a major, did not exist when they were in college.

The same was true for my wife's family, at least until we moved to Korea. My wife's mother (my mother-in-law) is notoriously hard to get along with. Where she goes, conflict ensues. She says the wrong things and upsets people. I am about the only person in the family who gets along fine with her. That is because I do not speak Korean, and she does not speak English. No doubt she says many mean and hurtful things to me, but I do not know what she is saying. I just smile back at her.

My mother-in-law creates much stress and drama in my wife's family. My wife attended college in America and was a professor of communication with me at Michigan State. Consequently, she had been away from Korea for many years. Then, Korea University recruited her. I was a spousal hire. When we moved to Korea, my wife had much more interaction with her family than she did when we lived in America. She quickly got drawn into the family dramas. After we moved there, the rest of the family started noticing how my wife interacted with her mother and how she navigated the dramas. Their reaction was, "Ah, we are starting to understand what communication is about." Competent communication has a "know it when you see it" quality. You do not need to understand it or even be able to do it well yourself to appreciate seeing it enacted by others. Recognizing it is one thing. Being able to do it is another.

Effectiveness and Competence

It is important to recognize the difference between effective communication and communication competence. The terms are sometimes used interchangeably. Being *effective* relates to accomplishing a goal. So, for example, if my goal is for you to understand the difference between effective communication and communication competence, I am effective to the extent that that goal is achieved, and you understand what I am trying to communicate. *Communication competence* is being a good communicator. Being effective—that is, accomplishing your desired communication goals—is part of competence, but there is more to it. **Competent communication also involves goal selection, goal prioritization, ethics, and aesthetics.** The competent communicator knows which goals to prioritize given the situation and does so elegantly and ethically. Someone could be ruthlessly effective but seldom ruthlessly competent.

Think about conflict situations. You can be effective in winning an argument when the better communication move is to pick your battles and let the issue go. Deception might be an even better example. You can do much harm to yourself and others by effectively deceiving people.

Communication competence has at least three broad sets of abilities or skills associated with it. First, the competent communicator is good at reading people and social situations. They are socially perceptive. Second, they use their social knowledge to say and do the right things. That is, they are good at message production. Third, they are also good at message reception. They are active listeners. They are attentive to others and good at understanding what others mean.

Two Approaches to Competence

In the field of communication, there are two main approaches to competence. The most common one often goes by the label *person-centered communication* and is often associated with the work of Brant Burleson, his colleagues, and his students. Person-centered messages are responsive to the communication situation, the subjective and emotional states of others, and the nature of the relationship between the communicators. In the context of providing emotional support, for example, on the low end of person-centeredness, other's feelings are ignored, dismissed, or criticized. My opening example of the boorish respondent was not at all person-centered. In highly person-centered messages, in contrast, other's feelings are recognized, validated, and elaborated upon. Research finds that the more highly person-centered a social support message is, the more effective it is in providing support.[1]

The other approach was advanced by my former professor, G. R. Miller, in his 1975 book *Between People*. We can call this second approach person-specific tailoring. The second approach thinks about communication competence as getting to know who you are talking to as a unique individual and then tailoring your message to them in a way that they appreciate.

Let me give you a personal example. Since coming to UAB, I have worked under and reported to two different deans. One was the dean who recruited and hired me, and the second was my new dean. The two have different backgrounds, personalities, communication styles, and priorities. Whichever dean I was reporting to, my

1. High and Dillard (2012).

effectiveness in my role as chair depended on figuring out an optimal approach to working with them. The faster I can do this and less trial and error the better.

The difference between the approaches is subtle but important. The person-centered approach considers the message given the situation. You do not need to know who the people are to know if a message is high in person-centeredness. Person-centeredness is in the message and situation. In Miller's approach, a low person-centered message could be competent with certain people.

At the beginning of the theory of mind chapter, I told the story of getting the rejection letter that read: "Dear Professor Levine, we had several good candidates. Unfortunately, you were not among them." This is extremely low in person-centeredness, and without knowing the people involved and the intricacies of context, this seems horribly incompetent (although brutally effective in communicating the rejection). However, from the second perspective, this can be thought of as competent given the situation and the people involved.

Another example is when my wife is complaining to me about something at her work. This is a social support situation, and I need to be supportive. How best to do this, however, involves choosing between three options. First, she might just be venting. If so, I need to listen attentively but not say much other than letting her know that I am listening carefully. Second, she might be looking for advice or seeking my reading of the situation. If so, I need to respond constructively with something helpful. Third, she might be looking for emotional support. If this is the case, then I need to respond with a highly person-centered message. Within a conversation, I might need to cycle between all three. The better I know and understand my wife, the better I can be supportive in the way she needs at each point in the interaction.

Nunchi

The Korean concept of *nunchi* (noon-chee) clarifies communication competence. It is a broad term involving being able to read a situation and people, anticipating what might happen or what might be needed, and saying and doing the right things. One of the things I liked about being a professor in Korea is that each professor had a teaching assistant. One of my assistants did not have much nunchi. She would ask me what I needed her to do. Another assistant of mine had nunchi. This assistant noticed, for example, my routine at the beginning of class and how I liked things set up. Before long, when I walked into class, things would be set up and ready to go, just as if I were doing it for myself.

Some of the Many Things That Contribute to Communication Competence

- Understand and appreciate the importance of social integration and the value of being well-networked. Make and maintain good connections with others.
- Understand and appreciate that communication is a process.
- Recognize the challenges in understanding another person, appreciate the potential for misunderstanding, and be cognizant of the idea that understanding is, at best, an approximation.
- Be ethical, and act in accordance with your values.
- Know the differences between issues of definition, fact, and value.
- Know your audience and adapt to them.
- Make and recognize sound and strong arguments.
- Establish your credibility as a communicator.
- Effectively use evidence and reason in persuasion.

- Be a literate consumer of persuasion by recognizing emotional appeals and compliance-gaining strategies.
- Manage how you present yourself nonverbally.
- Be aware that others' nonverbal communication can mean lots of different things.
- Maintain your own face and be respectful of other's face.
- Practice perspective taking and empathic concern; manage emotional contagion.
- Me mindful of cultural differences.
- Be open-minded.
- Treat others fairly and convey that.
- Learn to effectively deal with conflict.
- Practice packaged honesty and avoid lying when you can.

This concludes the last chapter. Dr. Shebib and I hope you enjoyed this book and found it informative and useful.

References

Ainsworth, M. D. S. (1969). Object relations, dependency, and attachment: A theoretical review of the infant-mother relationship. *Child Development, 40*(4), 969–1025. https://doi.org/10.2307/1127008

Ainsworth, M. D. S. (1982). Attachment: Retrospect and prospect. In C. M. Parkes & J. Stevenson-Hinde (eds.), *The place of attachment in human behavior* (pp. 3–30). Basic Books.

Ainsworth, M. D. S. (1989). Attachments beyond infancy. *American Psychologist, 44*(4), 709–716. https://doi.org/10.1037/0003-066X.44.4.709

Ainsworth, M. D. S., Bell, S. M., & Stayton, D. J. (1971). Individual differences in strange-situation behaviour of one-year-olds. In H. R. Schaffer (Ed.), *The origins of human social relations*. Academic Press.

Ainsworth, M. D. S., Blehar, M. C., Waters, E., & Wall, S. (1978). *Patterns of attachment: A psychological study of the strange situation*. Lawrence Erlbaum.

Ainsworth, M. D. S., & Eichberg, C. G. (1991). Effects on infant-mother attachment of mother's unresolved loss of an attachment figure, or other traumatic experience. In C. M. Parkes, J. Stevenson-Hinde, & P. Marris (Eds.), *Attachment across the life cycle* (pp. 160–183). Tavistock/Routledge.

Ainsworth, M. D. S., & Wittig, B. A. (1969). Attachment and exploratory behavior of one-year-olds in a strange situation. In B. M. Foss (Ed.), *Determinants of infant behavior* (Vol. 4, pp. 113–136). Methuen.

Alberts, J. K. (1988). An analysis of couples' conversational complaints. *Communication Monographs, 55*(2), 184–197. https://doi.org/10.1080/03637758809376165

Andersen, P. A. (1999). *Nonverbal communication: Forms and functions*. Mayfield.

Anderson, K. J., & Leaper, C. (1998). Meta-analyses of gender effects on conversational interruption: Who, what, when, where, and how? *Sex Roles, 39*, 225–252. https://doi.org/10.1023/A:1018802521676

Asch, S. E. (1956). Studies of independence and conformity: I. A minority of one against a unanimous majority. *Psychological Monographs: General and Applied, 70*(9), 1–70. https://doi.org/10.1037/h0093718

Bach, G. R., & Wyden, P. (1970). *The intimate enemy: How to fight fair in love and marriage*. Avon Books.

Baird, A. M., & Parayitam, S. (2019). Employers' ratings of importance of skills and competencies college graduates need to get hired: Evidence from the New England region of USA. *Education + Training, 61*, 622–634. https://doi.org/10.1108/et-12-2018-0250

Baxter, L. A., & Wilmot, W. W. (1984). "Secret tests": Social strategies for acquiring information about the state of the relationship. *Human Communication Research, 11*(2), 171–201. https://doi.org/10.1111/j.1468-2958.1984.tb00044.x

Beatty, M. J., Heisel, A. D., Hall, A. E., Levine, T. R., & LaFrance, B. H. (2002). What can we learn from the study of twins about genetic and environmental influences on interpersonal affiliation, aggressiveness, and social anxiety? A meta-analysis. *Communication Monographs, 69*, 1–18. https://doi.org/10.1080/03637750216534

Beatty, M. J., Heisel, A. D., Pascual-Ferra, P., & Berger, C. R. (2015). Electroencephalographic analysis in communication science: Testing two competing models of message production. *Communication Methods and Measures, 9*, 101–116. https://doi.org/10.1080/19312458.2014.999753

Bell, R. A., & Buerkel-Rothfuss, N. L. (1990). S(he) loves me, s(he) loves me not: Predictors of relational information-seeking in courtship and beyond. *Communication Quarterly, 38*, 64–82. https://doi.org/10.1080/01463379009369742

Bem, S. L. (1974). The measurement of psychological androgyny. *Journal of Consulting and Clinical Psychology, 42*(2), 155–162. https://doi.org/10.1037/h0036215

Bem, S. L. (1978). *Bem sex-role inventory: Professional manual*. Consulting Psychology Press.

Berger, C. R. (1979). Beyond initial interaction: Uncertainty, understanding, and the development of interpersonal relationships. In H. Giles & R. N. St. Clair (Eds.), *Language and social psychology* (pp. 122–144). Basil Blackwell.

Berger, C. R. (1987). Communicating under uncertainty. In M. E. Roloff & G. R. Miller (Eds.), *Interpersonal processes: New directions in communication research* (pp. 39–62). SAGE Publications.

Berger, C. R., & Calabrese, R. J. (1975). Some explorations in initial interactions and beyond: Toward a developmental theory of interpersonal communication. *Human Communication Research, 1*(2), 99–112. https://doi.org/10.1111/j.1468-2958.1975.tb00258.x

Berger, C. R., & di Battista, P. (2009). Communication failure and plan adaptation: If at first you don't succeed, say it louder and slower. *Communication Monographs, 60*, 220–238. https://doi.org/10.1080/03637759309376310

Berlo, D. K. (1960). *The process of communication*. Thomson.

Bettencourt, B. A., & Miller, N. (1996). Gender differences in aggression as a function of provocation: A meta-analysis. *Psychological Bulletin*, *119*(3), 422–447. https://doi.org/10.1037/0033-2909.119.3.422

Bisson, M. A., & Levine, T. R. (2009). Negotiating a friends with benefits relationship. *Archives of Sexual Behavior, 38*, 66–73. https://doi.org/10.1007/s10508-007-9211-2

Bolkan, S., Griffin, D. J., Holmgren, J. L., & Hickson, M., III (2012). Prolific scholarship in communication studies: Five years in review. *Communication Education, 61*, 380–394. https://doi.org/10.1080/03634523.2012.699080

Bond, C. F., Jr., & DePaulo, B. M. (2006). Accuracy of deception judgments. *Personality and Social Psychology Review, 10*, 214–234. https://doi.org/10.1207/s15327957pspr1003_2

Bond, C. F., & The Global Deception Research Team (2006). A world of lies. *Journal of Cross-Cultural Psychology, 37*, 60–74.

Bornstein, R. F. (1989). Exposure and affect: Overview and meta-analysis of research, 1968–1987. *Psychological Bulletin, 106*(2), 265–289. https://doi.org/10.1037/0033-2909.106.2.265

Boster, F. J., & Mongeau, P. (1984). Fear-arousing persuasive messages. *Annals of the International Communication Association, 8*, 330–375. https://doi.org/10.1080/23808985.1984.11678581

Boster, F. J., Shaw, A. S., Hughes, M, Kotowski, M. R., Strom, R. E., & Deatrick, L. M. (2009). Dump-and-chase: The effectiveness of persistence as a sequential request compliance-gaining strategy. *Communication Studies, 60*, 219–234. https://doi.org/10.1080/10510970902955976

Bowlby, J. (1973). *Attachment and loss. Vol 2: Separation: Anxiety and anger*. Basic Books.

Bowlby, J. (1977). The making and breaking of affectional bonds: I. Aetiology and psychopathology in the light of attachment theory. *The British Journal of Psychiatry*, *130*, 201–210. https://doi.org/10.1192/bjp.130.3.201

Bowlby, J. (1982). Attachment and loss: Retrospect and prospect. *American Journal of Orthopsychiatry, 52*(4), 664–678. https://doi.org/10.1111/j.1939-0025.1982.tb01456.x

Bowling, A. (1995). What are the important things in people's lives? A survey of the publics judgements to inform scales of health related quality of life. *Social Science and Medicine, 41*, 1447–1462. https://doi.org/10.1016/0277-9536(95)00113-l

Brehm, J. W. (1966). *A theory of psychological reactance*. Academic Press.

Bretherton, I., & Munholland, K. A. (2008). Internal working models in attachment relationships: Elaborating a central construct in attachment theory. In J. Cassidy & P. R. Shaver (Eds.), *Handbook of attachment: Theory, research, and clinical applications* (2nd ed., pp. 102–127). The Guilford Press.

Brynes, J. P., Miller, D. C., & Schafer, W. D. (1999). Gender differences in risk taking: A meta-analysis. *Psychological Bulletin, 125*(3), 367–383. https://doi.org/10.1037/0033-2909.125.3.367

Buller, D. B., & Aune, R. K. (1988). The effects of vocalics and nonverbal sensitivity on compliance: A speech accommodation theory explanation. *Human Communication Research, 14*, 301–332. https://doi.org/10.1111/j.1468-2958.1988.tb00159.x

Burger, J. M. (1986). Increasing compliance by improving the deal: The that's-not-all technique. *Journal of Personality and Social Psychology, 51*, 277–283. https://doi.org/10.1037/0022-3514.51.2.277

Burger, J. M., & Shelton, M. (2011). Changing everyday health behaviors through descriptive norm manipulations. *Social Influence, 6*(2), 69–77. https://doi.org/10.1080/15534510.2010.542305

Burgoon, J. K., Buller, D. B., & Woodall, W. G. (1996). *Nonverbal communication: The unspoken dialogue* (3rd ed.). McGraw-Hill.

Burgoon, J. K., Guerrero, L. K., & Floyd, K. (2010). *Nonverbal communication*. Pearson.

Buss, D. M., & Barnes, M. (1986). Preferences in human mate selection. *Journal of Personality and Social Psychology, 50*(3), 559–570. https://doi.org/10.1037/0022-3514.50.3.559

Cacioppo, J. T., Gardner, W. L., & Berntson, G. G. (1999). The affect system has parallel and integrative processing components: Form follows function. *Journal of Personality and Social Psychology, 76*(5), 839–855. https://doi.org/10.1037/0022-3514.76.5.839

Cacioppo, J. T., & Patrick, W. (2008). *Loneliness: Human nature and the need for social connection*. Norton.

Cacioppo, J. T., & Petty, R. E. (1982). The need for cognition. *Journal of Personality and Social Psychology, 42*(1), 116–131. https://doi.org/10.1037/0022-3514.42.1.116

Canary, D. J., Cupach, W. R., & Messman, S. J. (1995). *Relationship conflict*. SAGE Publications.

Carpenter, C. J. (2012). A meta-analysis of the effectiveness of the "but you are free" compliance-gaining technique. *Communication Studies, 64*, 6–17. https://doi/org/10.1080/10510974.2012.727941

Carver, C. S., & Scheier, M. F. (1990). Origins and functions of positive and negative affect: A control-process view. *Psychological Review, 97*(1), 19–35. https://doi.org/10.1037/0033-295X.97.1.19

Cialdini, R. B. (2021). *Influence: The psychology of persuasion*. Harper.

Cialdini, R. B., Cacioppo, J. T., Bassett, R., & Miller, J. A. (1978). Low-ball procedure for producing compliance: Commitment then cost. *Journal of Personality and Social Psychology, 36*, 463–476. https://doi.org/10.1037/0022-3514.36.5.463

Cialdini, R. B., & Schroeder, D. A. (1976). Increasing compliance by legitimizing paltry contributions: When even a penny helps. *Journal of Personality and Social Psychology, 34*, 599–604. https://doi.org/10.1037/0022-3514.34.4.599

Cialdini, R. B., Vincent, J. E., Lewis, S. K., Catalan, J., Wheeler, D., & Darby, B. L. (1975). Reciprocal concessions procedure for inducing compliance: The door-in-the-face technique. *Journal of Personality and Social Psychology, 31*(2), 206–215. https://doi.org/10.1037/h0076284

Christensen, A., & Heavey, C. L. (1990). Gender and social structure in the demand/withdraw pattern of marital conflict. *Journal of Personality & Social Psychology, 59*(1), 73–81. https://doi.org/10.1037/0022-3514.59.1.73

Collins, N. L., & Read, S. J. (1994). Cognitive representations of attachment: The structure and function of working models. In K. Bartholomew & D. Perlman (Eds.), *Attachment processes in adulthood* (pp. 53–90). Jessica Kingsley Publishers.

Costa, D. L., & Kahn, M. E. (2010). Energy conservation "nudges" and environmentalist ideology: Evidence from a randomized residential electricity field experiment. *Journal of the European Economic Association, 11*(3), 680–702. https://doi.org/10.1111/jeea.12011

Davis, B. P., & Knowles, E. S. (1999). A disrupt-then-reframe technique of social influence. *Journal of Personality and Social Psychology, 76,* 192–199. https://doi.org/10.1037/0022-3514.76.2.192

Dawkins, R. (2016). *The selfish gene* (4th ed.). Oxford University Press.

de Hoog, N., Stroebe, W., & de Wit, J. B. F. (2007). The impact of vulnerability to and severity of a health risk on processing and acceptance of fear-arousing communications: A meta-analysis. *Review of General Psychology, 11*(3), 258–285. https://doi.org/10.1037/1089-2680.11.3.258

de Hoog, N., Stroebe, W., & de Wit, J. B. F. (2008). The processing of fear-arousing communications: How biased processing leads to persuasion. *Social Influence, 3,* 84–113. https://doi.org/10.1080/15534510802185836

DePaulo, B. M., Lindsay, J. J., Malone, B. E., Muhlenbruck, L., Charlton, K., & Cooper, H. (2003). Cues to deception. *Psychological Bulletin, 129,* 74–118. https://doi.org/10.1037/0033-2909.129.1.74

Dillard, J. P., Hunter, J. E., & Burgoon, M. (1984). Sequential-request persuasive strategies: Meta-analysis of foot-in-the-door and door-in-the-face. *Human Communication Research, 10,* 461–488. https://doi.org/10.1111/j.1468-2958.1984.tb00028.x

Dillard, J. P., & Pfau, M. (2002). *The persuasion handbook: Developments in theory and practice.* SAGE Publications.

Dindia, K., & Allen, M. (1992). Sex differences in self-disclosure: A meta-analysis. *Psychology Bulletin, 112*(1), 106–124. https://doi.org/10.1037/0033-2909.112.1.106

Dion, K., Berscheid, E., & Walster, E. (1972). What is beautiful is good. *Journal of Personality and Social Psychology, 24*(3), 285–290. https://doi.org/10.1037/h0033731

Douglas, W. (1990). Uncertainty, information-seeking, and liking during initial interaction. *Western Journal of Speech Communication, 54,* 66–81. https://doi.org/10.1080/10570319009374325

Driscoll, R., Davis, K. E., & Lipetz, M. E. (1972). Parental interference and romantic love: The Romeo and Juliet effect. *Journal of Personality and Social Psychology, 24,* 1–10. https://doi.org/10.1037/h0033373

Duff, D. C., Levine, T. R., Beatty, M. J., Woobright, J, & Park, H. S. (2007). Testing public anxiety treatments against a credible placebo control. *Communication Education, 56,* 72–88. https://doi.org/10.1080/03634520601016186

Eagly, A. H., & Johnson, B. T. (1990). Gender and leadership style: A meta-analysis. *Psychological Bulletin, 108*(2), 233–256. https://doi.org/10.1037/0033-2909.108.2.233

Eagly, A. H., Karau, S. J., & Makhijani, M. G. (1995). Gender and the effectiveness of leaders: A meta-analysis. *Psychological Bulletin, 117*(1), 125–145. https://doi.org/10.1037/0033-2909.117.1.125

Ekman, P. (2003). *Emotions revealed: Recognizing faces and feelings to improve communication and emotional life.* Times Books/Henry Holt and Co.

Ekman, P., & Friesen, W. V. (1969). The repertoire of nonverbal behavior: Categories, origins, usage, and coding. *Semiotica, 1,* 49–98. https://doi.org/10.1515/semi.1969.1.1.49

Ekman, P., Levenson, R. W., & Friesen, W. V. (1983). Autonomic nervous system activity distinguishes among emotions. *Science, 221,* 1208–1210. https://doi.org/10.1126/science.6612338

Feeley, T. H., Anker, A. E., & Aloe, A. M. (2012). The door-in-the-face persuasive message strategy: A meta-analysis of the first 35 years. *Communication Monographs, 79,* 316–343. https://doi.org/10.1080/03637751.2012.697631

Fitzpatrick, M. A., & Ritchie, L. D. (1994). Communication schemata within the family: Multiple perspectives on family interaction. *Human Communication Research, 20,* 275–301. https://doi.org/10.1111/j.1468-2958.1994.tb00324.x

Forgas, J. P. (1995). Mood and judgment: The affect infusion model (AIM). *Psychological Bulletin, 117*(1), 39–66. https://doi.org/10.1037/0033-2909.117.1.39

Freedman, J. L., & Fraser, S. C. (1966). Compliance without pressure: The foot-in-the-door technique. *Journal of Personality and Social Psychology, 4,* 195–202. https://doi.org/10.1037/h0023552

Gasiorek, J., & Aune, R. K. (2021). *Creating Understanding.* Peter Lang.

Giles, H., & Wiemann, J. M. (1987). Language, social comparison, and power. In C. R. Berger & S. H. Chaffee (Eds.), *The Handbook of Communication Science* (pp. 350–384). SAGE Publications.

Gladwell, M. (2002). *The tipping point: How little things can make a big difference.* Back Bay Books.

Goei, R., Massi Lindsey, L. L., Boster, F. J., Skalski, P. D., & Bowman, J. M. (2003). The mediating roles of liking and obligation on the relationship between favors and compliance. *Communication Research, 30,* 178–197. https://doi.org/10.1177/0093650202250877

Gottman, J. M. (1994). *What predicts divorce? The relationship between marital processes and marital outcomes.* Lawrence Erlbaum Associates.

Gottman Institute. (2023). https://www.gottman.com

Gouldner, A. W. (1960). The norm of reciprocity: A preliminary statement. *American Sociological Review, 25*(2), 161–178. https://doi.org/10.2307/2092623

Guéguen, N., Jacob, C., & Boulbry, G. (2007). The effect of touch on compliance with a restaurant's employee suggestion. *Hospitality Management, 26,* 1019–1023. https://doi.org/10.1016/j.ijhm.2006.12.004

Haidt, J. (2013). *The righteous mind: Why good people are divided by politics and religion.* Vingage.

Hall, E. T. (1959). *The silent language.* Anchor/Doubleday.

Hall, E. T. (1990). *The hidden dimension* (2nd ed.). Anchor Press.

Harari, Y. N. (2015). *Sapiens: A brief history of humankind.* Harper.

Harlow, H. F. (1958). The nature of love. *American Psychologist, 13,* 673–685. https://doi.org/10.1037/h0047884

Harlow, H. F., Harlow, M. K., & Hansen, E. W. (1963). The maternal affectional system of rhesus monkeys. In H. L. Rheingold (Ed.), *Maternal behaviors in mammals* (pp. 254–281). John Wiley & Sons.

Harlow, H. F., & Zimmerman, R. R. (1958). The development of affectional responses in infant monkeys. *Proceedings of the American Philosophical Society, 102,* 501–509. https://www.jstor.org/stable/985597

Heider, F. (1946). Attitudes and cognitive organization. *Journal of Psychology, 21,* 107–112. https://doi.org/10.1080/00223980.1946.9917275

Heider, F. (1958). *The psychology of interpersonal relationships.* Wiley.

Hensley, W. E. (1981). The effects of attire, location, and sex on aiding behavior: A similarity explanation. *Journal of Nonverbal Behavior, 6,* 3–11. https://doi.org/10.1007/BF00987932

Hewes, D. E., Graham, M. L., Doelger, J., & Pavitt, C. (1985). "Second-guessing": Message interpretation in social networks. *Human Communication Research, 11,* 299–334. https://doi.org/10.1111/j.1468-2958.1985.tb00050.x

High, A. C., & Dillard, J. P. (2012) A review and meta-analysis of person-centered messages and social support outcomes, *Communication Studies, 63,* 99–118. https://doi.org/10.1080/10510974.2011.598208

Hinkle, L. L. (2001). Perceptions of supervisor nonverbal immediacy, vocalics, and subordinate liking. *Communication Research Reports, 18,* 128–136. https://doi.org/10.1080/08824090109384790

Hofstede, G. (2001). *Culture's consequences.* SAGE Publications.

Holmstrom, A. J., & Burleson, B. R. (2011). An initial test of a cognitive-emotional theory of esteem support messages. *Communication Research, 38,* 326–355. https://doi.org/10.1177/0093650210376191

Holt-Lunstad J., & Smith T. B. (2010) Social relationships and mortality risk: A meta-analytic review. *PLoS Medice, 7,* e1000316. https://doi.org/10.4016/19911.01

Holt-Lunstad, J., Smith, T. B., Baker, M., Harris, T., & Stephenson, D. (2015). Loneliness and social isolation as risk factors for mortality: A meta-analytic review. *Perspectives in Psychological Science, 10,* 227–237. https://doi.org/10.1177/1745691614568352

Hovland, C. I., & Weiss, W. (1951). The influence of source credibility on communication effectiveness. *Public Opinion Quarterly, 15,* 635–650. https://doi.org/10.1086/266350

Hornick, J. (1992). Tactile stimulation and consumer response. *Journal of Consumer Research, 19,* 449–458. https://doi.org/10.1086/209314

Imhof, M. (2010). Listening to voices and judging people. *International Journal of Listening, 24,* 19–33. https://doi.org/10.1080/10904010903466295

Johnson, B. T., & Eagly, A. H. (1989). Effects of involvement on persuasion: A meta-analysis. *Psychology Bulletin, 106*(2), 290–314. https://doi.org/10.1037/0033-2909.106.2.290

Jones, E. E., & Nisbett, R. E. (1971). *The actor and the observer: Divergent perceptions of the causes of behaviors.* General Learning Press.

Kellermann, K. A. (1995). The conversation MOP: A model of patterned and pliable behavior. In D. E. Hewes (Ed.), *The cognitive bases of interpersonal communication* (pp. 181–224). Lawrence Erlbaum.

Kiecolt-Glaser, J. K., & Newton, T. L. (2001). Marriage and health: his and hers. *Psychological bulletin, 127*(4), 472–503. https://doi.org/10.1037/0033-2909.127.4.472

Kleinke, C. L. (1980). Interaction between gaze and legitimacy of request on compliance in a field setting. *Journal of Nonverbal Behavior, 5,* 3–12. https://doi.org/10.1007/BF00987050

Knapp, M. L. (1992). *Nonverbal communication in human interaction* (3rd ed.). Holt, Rinehart, Winston.

Koerner, A. F., & Fitzpatrick, M. A. (2002a). Toward a theory of family communication. *Communication Theory, 12,* 70–91. https://doi.org/10.1111/comt.2002.12.issue-1

Koerner, A. F., & Fitzpatrick, M. A. (2002b). Understanding family communication patterns and family functioning: The roles of conversation orientation and conformity orientation. *Communication Yearbook, 26,* 37–69. https://doi.org/10.1080/23808985.2002.11679010

Koerner, A. F., & Fitzpatrick, M. A. (2006a). Family communication patterns theory: A social cognitive approach. In D. O. Braithwaite & L. A. Baxter (Eds.), *Engaging theories in family communication: Multiple perspectives* (pp. 50–65). SAGE Publications.

Koerner, A. F., & Fitzpatrick, M. A. (2006b). Family conflict communication. In J. G. Oetzel & S. Ting-Toomey (Eds.), *The SAGE handbook of conflict communication: Integrating theory, research, and practice* (pp. 159–183). SAGE Publications.

Koerner, A. F., & Schrodt, P. (2014). An introduction to the special issue on family communication patterns theory. *Journal of Family Communication, 14,* 1–15. https://doi.org/10.1080/15267431.2013.857328

Krumhuber, E., Manstead, A. S. R., & Kappas, A. (2007). Temporal aspects of facial displays in person and expression perception: The effects of smile dynamics, head-tilt, and gender. *Journal of Nonverbal Behavior, 31,* 39–56. https://doi.org/10.1007/s10919-006-0019-x

LaFrance, M., Hecht, M. A., & Paluck, E. L. (2003). The contingent smile: A meta-analysis of sex differences in smiling. *Psychological Bulletin, 129*(2), 305–334. https://doi.org/10.1037/0033-2909.129.2.305

Langer, E. J., Blank, A., & Chanowitz, B. (1978). The mindlessness of ostensibly thoughtful action: The role of "placebic" information in interpersonal interaction. *Journal of Personality and Social Psychology, 36,* 635–642. https://doi.org/10.1037/0022-3514.36.6.635

Ledbetter, A. M. (2019). Parent-child privacy boundary conflict patterns during the first year of college: Mediating family communication patterns, predicting psychosocial distress. *Human Communication Research, 45,* 255–285. https://doi.org/10.1093/hcr/hqy018

Levine, T. R. (2020). *Duped: Truth-default theory and the social science of lying and deception.* University of Alabama Press.

Levine, T. R., & Blair, J. P. (2018). Accurate expert deception detection: Faulty premises in Vrij et al. (2015). *Journal of Media and Communication Studies, 10,* 8–13. https://doi.org/10.5897/jmcs2017.0588

Levine, T. R., Blair, J. P. & Carpenter, C. J. (2018). A critical look at meta-analytic evidence for the cognitive approach to lie detection: A re-examination of Vrij, Fisher, and Blank (2017). *Legal and Criminological Psychology, 23,* 7–19. https://doi.org/10.1111/lcrp.12115

Levine, T. R., & Boster, F. J. (1996). The impact of self and other's argumentativeness on talk about controversial issues. *Communication Quarterly, 44,* 345–358. https://doi.org/10.1080/01463379609370022

Levine, T. R., & Boster, F. J. (2001). The effects of power and message variables on compliance. *Communication Monographs, 68,* 28–48. https://doi.org/10.1080/03637750128049

Levine, T., R., Bresnahan, M., Park, H. S., Lapinski, M. K., Lee, T. S., & Lee, D. W. (2003). The (in)validity of self-construal scales revisited. *Human Communication Research, 29,* 291–308. https://doi.org/10.1111/j.1468-2958.2003.tb00840.x

Levine, T. R., Kotowski, M. R., Beatty, M. J., & Van Kelegom, M. J. (2012). A meta-analysis of trait-behavior correlations in argumentativeness and verbal aggression. *Journal of Language and Social Psychology, 31,* 95–111. https://doi.org/10.1177/0261927x11425037

Levine, T. R., & McCornack, S. A. (1996). Can behavioral adaption explain the probing effect? *Human Communication Research, 22,* 603–612. https://doi.org/10.1111/j.1468-2958.1996.tb00382.x

Levine, T. R., & McCroskey, J. C. (1990). Measuring trait communication apprehension: A test of rival measurement models of the PRCA-24. *Communication Monographs, 57,* 62–72. https://doi.org/10.1080/03637759009376185

Levine, T. R., & Park, H. S. (2017). The researcher of James C. McCroskey: A personal and professional remembrance. *Communication Research Reports, 34,* 376–380. https://doi.org/10.1080/08824096.2017.1368474

Levine, T. R., Serota, K. B. Shulman, H., Clare, D. D., Park, H. S., Shaw, A. S., Shim, J. C., & Lee, J. H. (2011). Sender demeanor: Individual differences in sender believability have a powerful impact on deception detection judgments. *Human Communication Research, 37,* 377–403. https://doi.org/10.1111/j.1468-2958.2011.01407.x

Levine, T. R., Weber, R., Hullett, C. R., Park, H. S., & Lindsey, L. (2008). A critical assessment of null hypothesis significance testing in quantitative communication research. *Human Communication Research, 34,* 171–187. https://doi.org/10.1111/j.1468-2958.2008.00317.x

Lubinski, D. (2004). Introduction to the special section on cognitive abilities: 100 years after Spearman's (1904) "'general intelligence,' objectively determined and measured." *Journal of Personality and Social Psychology, 86,* 96–111. https://doi.org/10.1037/0022-3514.86.1.96

Markus, H. R., & Kitayama, S. (1991). Culture and the self: Implications for cognition, emotion, and motivation. *Psychological Review, 98,* 224–253. https://doi.org/10.1037/0033-295X.98.2.224

Maslow, A. H. (1943). A theory of human motivation. *Psychological Review, 50(4),* 370–396. https://doi.org/10.1037/h0054346

Maslow, A. H. (1954). *Motivation and personality.* Harper and Row.

Mehl, M. R., Vazire, S., Ramírez-Esparza, N., Slatcher, R. B., & Pennebaker, J. W. (2007). Are women really more talkative than men? *Science, 317(5834),* 82. https://doi.org/10.1126/science.1139940

McCornack, S. A. (1992). Information manipulation theory. *Communication Monographs, 59,* 1–16. https://doi.org/10.1080/03637759209376245

McCornack, S. A. (1997). The generation of deceptive messages: Laying the groundwork for a viable theory of interpersonal deception. In J. O. Greene (Ed.), *Message production: Advances in communication theory* (pp. 91–126). Erlbaum.

McCornack, S. A., Levine, T. R., Morrison, K., & Lapinski, M. (1996). Speaking of information manipulation: A critical rejoinder. *Communication Monographs, 63,* 83–91. https://doi.org/10.1080/03637759609376376

McCornack, S.A., Morrison, K., Paik, J. E., Wiser, A. M., & Zhu, X. (2014). Information manipulation theory 2: A propositional theory of deceptive discourse production. *Journal of Language and Social Psychology, 33,* 348–377. https://doi.org/10.1177/0261927X14534656

McCornack, S. A., & Parks, M. R. (1986). Deception detection and relationship development: The other side of trust. *Annals of the International Communication Association, 9,* 377–389. https://doi.org/10.1080/23808985.1986.11678616

McCrae, R. R., & Costa, P. T. Jr. (1987). Validation of the five-factor model of personality across instruments and observers. *Journal of Personality and Social Psychology, 52,* 81–90.

McCroskey, J. C. (1969). A summary of experimental research on the effects of evidence in persuasive communication. *The Quarterly Journal of Speech, 55,* 169–176. https://doi.org/10.1080/00335636909382942

McCroskey, J. C., & Daly, J. A. (1987). *Personality and interpersonal communication.* SAGE Publications.

Milgram, S. (1963). Behavioral Study of obedience. *The Journal of Abnormal and Social Psychology, 67(4),* 371–378. https://doi.org/10.1037/h0040525

Miller, G. R., Boster, F., Roloff, M., & Seibold, D. (1977). Compliance-gaining message strategies: A typology and some findings concerning effects of situational differences. *Communication Monographs, 44,* 37–51. https://doi.org/10.1080/03637757709390113

Miller, G. R., & Nicholson, H. E. (1976). *Communication inquiry: A perspective on a process.* Addison-Westly.

Miller, G. R., & Steinberg, M. (1975). *Between people: A new analysis of interpersonal communication.* Science Research Associates.

Miller, N., Maruyama, G., Beaber, R. J., & Valone, K. (1976). Speed of speech and persuasion. *Journal of Personality and Social Psychology, 34,* 615–624. https://doi.org/10.1037/0022-3514.34.4.615

Moore, D. W. (2003, January 3). *Family, health most important aspects of life. Gallop Poll Press Release.* https://news.gallup.com/poll/7504/family-health-most-important-aspects-life.aspx

Morris, K. A., & Swann, W. B., Jr. (1996). Denial and the AIDS crisis: On wishing away the threat of AIDS. In S. Oskamp & S. C. Thompson (Eds.), *Understanding and preventing HIV risk behavior: Safer sex and drug use* (pp. 57–79). SAGE Publications.

NACE. (2020). *Key attributes employers want to see on students' resumes.* https://www.naceweb.org/talent-acquisition/candidate-selection/key-attributes-employers-want-to-see-on-students-resumes/

Newcomb, T. M. (1953). An approach to the study of communicative acts. *Psychology Review, 60,* 393–404. https://doi.org/10.1037/h0063098

O'Keefe, D. J., & Hale, S. L. (2009). An odds-ratio-based meta-analysis of research on the door- in-the-face influence strategy. *Communication Reports, 14,* 31–38. https://doi.org/10.1080/08934210109367734

Oliver, M. B., & Hyde, J. S. (1993). Gender differences in sexuality: A meta-analysis. *Psychological Bulletin, 114(1),* 29–51. https://doi.org/10.1037/0033-2909.114.1.29

Oyserman, D., Coon, H. M., & Kemmelmeier, M. (2002). Rethinking individualism and collectivism: Evaluation of theoretical assumptions and meta-analyses. *Psychological Bulletin, 128,* 3–72. https://doi.org/10.1037/0033-2909.128.1.3

Park, H. S., & Levine, T. R. (2015). Base-rates, deception detection, and deception theory: A reply to Burgoon (2015). *Human Communication Research, 41,* 350–366. https://doi.org/10.1111/hcre.12066

Parks, M. R., & Adelman, M. B. (1983). Communication networks and the development of romantic relationships: An expansion of uncertainty reduction theory. *Human Communication Research, 10,* 55–79. https://doi.org/10.1111/j.1468-2958.1983.tb00004.x

Patterson, M. L., Powell, J. L., & Lenihan, M. G. (1986). Touch, compliance and interpersonal affect. *Journal of Nonverbal Behavior, 10,* 41–50. https://doi.org/10.1007/BF00987204

Petty, R. E., & Cacioppo, J. T. (1986a). *Communication and persuasion: Central and peripheral routes to attitude change.* Springer-Verlag.

Petty, R. E., & Cacioppo, J. T. (1986b). The elaboration likelihood model of persuasion. *Advances in Experimental Social Psychology, 19,* 123–205. https://doi.org/10.1007/978-1-4612-4964-1_1

Paulhus, D. L., & Williams, K. M. (2002). The dark triad of personality: Narcissism, Machiavellianism, and psychopathy. *Journal of Research in Personality, 36,* 556–563. https://doi.org/10.1016/0022-1031(71)90025-4563

Reinsch, N., L. Jr., & Gardner, J. A. (2014). Do communication abilities affect promotion decisions? Some data from the c-suit. *Journal of Business and Technical Communication, 28,* 31–57. https://doi.org/10.1177/1050651913502357

Reite, M. (1990). Touch, attachment, and health: Is there a relationship? In K. E. Barnard & T. B. Brazelton (Eds.), *Touch: The foundation of experience: Full revised and expanded proceedings of Johnson & Johnson Pediatric Round Table X. Clinical infant reports* (pp. 195–225). International Universities Press.

Reese-Weber, M., & Bartle-Haring, S. (1998). Conflict resolution styles in family subsystems and adolescent romantic relationships. *Journal of Youth and Adolescence, 27*(6), 735–752. https://doi.org/10.1023/A:1022861832406

Regan, D. T. (1971). Effects of a favor and liking on compliance. *Journal of Experimental Social Psychology, 7,* 627–639. https://doi.org/10.1016/0022-1031(71)90025-4

Ritchie, L. D., & Fitzpatrick, M. A. (1990). Family communication patterns: Measuring intrapersonal perceptions of interpersonal relationships. *Communication Research, 17,* 523–544. https://doi.org/10.1177/009365090017004007

Rogers, E. M. (2003). *Diffusion of innovations.* Free Press.

Rogers, R. W., & Prentice-Dunn, S. (1997). Protection motivation theory. In D. S. Gochman (Ed.), *Handbook of health behavior research 1: Personal and social determinants* (pp. 113–132). Plenum Press.

Rokeach, M. (1960). *The open and closed mind.* Basic Books.

Saigh, P. A. (1981). Effects of nonverbal examiner praise on selected WAIS subtest performance of Lebanese undergraduates. *Journal of Nonverbal Behavior, 6,* 84–86. https://doi.org/10.1007/BF00987283

Schwab, C. (2020). *Modern wealth survey.* https://content.schwab.com/web/retail/public/about-schwab/charles-schwab-modern-wealth-survey-2020-phoenix.pdf, https://content.schwab.com/web/retail/public/about-schwab/charles-schwab-modern-wealth-survey-2020-washington-dc.pdf, https://content.schwab.com/web/retail/public/about-schwab/charles-schwab-modern-wealth-survey-2020-los-angeles-and-orange-county.pdf

Segrin, C. (1993). The effects of nonverbal behavior on outcomes of compliance gaining attempts. *Communication Studies, 44,* 169–187. https://doi.org/10.1080/10510979309368393

Sillars, A. L., Pike, G. P., Jones, T. S., & Murphy, M. A. (1984). Communication and understanding in marriage. *Human Communication Research, 10,* 317–350. https://doi.org/10.1111/j.1468-2958.1984.tb00022.x

Simonds, B. K., Meyer, K. R., Quinlan, M. M., & Hunt, S. (2006). Effects of instructor speech rate on student affective learning, recall, and perceptions of nonverbal immediacy, credibility, and clarity. *Communication Research Reports, 23,* 187–197. https://doi.org/10.1080/08824090600796401

Sillars, A. L. (1980). Attributions and communication in roommate conflict. *Communication Monographs, 47,* 180–200. https://doi.org/10.1080/03637758009376031

Sinclair, H. C., Hood, K. B., & Wright, B. L. (2014). Revisiting the Romeo and Juliet effect: Reexamining the links between social network opinions and romantic relationship outcomes. *Social Psychology, 45,* 170–178. https://doi.org/10.1027/1864-9335/a000181

Shebib, S. J., Holmstrom, A. J., Mason, A. J., Mazur, A. P., Zhang, L., & Allard, A. (2020). Sex and gender differences in esteem support: Examining main and interaction effects. *Communication Studies, 71*(1), 167–186. https://doi.org/10.1080/10510974.2019.1692886

Sherif, M., & Hovland, C. I. (1961). *Social judgement.* Yale University Press.

Stern, S. E., Mullennix, J. W., Dyson, C., & Wilson, S. J. (1999). The persuasiveness of synthetic speech versus human speech. *Human Factors, 41*(4), 588–595. https://doi.org/10.1518/001872099779656680

Strohmetz, D. B., Rind, B., Fisher, R., & Lynn, M. (2002). Sweetening the till: The use of candy to increase restaurant tipping. *Journal of Applied Social Psychology, 32*(2), 300–309. https://doi.org/10.1111/j.1559-1816.2002.tb00216.x

Tesser, A. (1978). Self-generated attitude change. In L. Berkowitz (Ed.), *Advances in experimental social psychology* (Vol. 11, pp. 229–338). Academic Press.

Tidd, K. L., & Lockard, J. S. (1978). Monetary significance of the affiliative smile: A case for reciprocal altruism. *Bulletin of the Psychonomic Society, 11*(6), 344–346. https://doi.org/10.3758/BF03336849

Trimpop, R. (1994). *The psychology of risk taking behavior.* Elsevier Science.

Thomas, L. T., & Levine, T. R. (1994). Disentangling listening and memory: Related but separate constructs? *Human Communication Research, 21,* 103–127. https://doi.org/10.1111/j.1468-2958.1994.tb00342.x

Thomas, L. T., & Levine, T. R. (1996). Further thoughts on recall, memory, and the measurement of listening: A rejoinder to Bostrom. *Human Communication Research, 23,* 306–308. https://doi.org/10.1111/j.1468-2958.1996.tb00397.x

Vaidis, D. C. F., & Halimi-Falkowicz, S. G. M. (2008). Increasing compliance with a request: Two touches are more effective than one. *Psychological Reports, 103,* 88–92. https://doi.org/10.2466/pr0.103.1.88-92

Watson, D., Wiese, D., Vaidya, J., & Tellegen, A. (1999). The two general activation systems of affect: Structural findings, evolutionary considerations, and psychobiological evidence. *Journal of Personality and Social Psychology, 76*(5), 820–838. https://doi.org/10.1037/0022-3514.76.5.820

Weber, R., Huskey, R., & Mangus, J. M. (2014). Neural predictors of message effectiveness during counterarguing in antidrug campaigns. *Communication Monographs, 82,* 4–30. https://doi.org/10.1080/03637751.2014.971414

Weinstein, N. D. (1980). Unrealistic optimism about future life events. *Journal of Personality and Social Psychology, 39,* 806–820. https://doi.org/10.1037/0022-3514.39.5.806

Weinstein, N. D. (1993). Testing four competing theories of health-protective behavior. *Health Psychology, 12,* 324–333. https://doi.org/10.1037//0278-6133.12.4.324

Willis, F. N., & Hamm, H. K. (1980). The use of interpersonal touch in securing compliance. *Journal of Nonverbal Behavior, 5,* 49–55. https://doi.org/10.1007/BF00987054

Wilmot, W., & Hocker, J. (2013). *Interpersonal conflict* (9th ed.). McGraw Hill.

Witte, K. (1994). Fear control and danger control: A test of the extended parallel process model (EPPM). *Communication Monographs, 61*(2), 113–134. https://doi.org/10.1080/03637759409376328

Witte, K., Cameron, K. A., McKeon, J. K., & Berkowitz, J. M. (1996). Predicting risk behaviors: Development and validation of a diagnostic scale. *Journal of Health Communication, 1*(4), 317–341. https://doi.org/10.1080/108107396127988

Zajonc, R. B. (1968). Attitudinal effects of mere exposure. *Journal of Personality and Social Psychology, 9*(2, Pt.2), 1–27. https://doi.org/10.1037/h0025848

Zuckerman, M., & Driver, R. E. (1989). What sounds beautiful is good: The vocal attractiveness stereotype. *Journal of Nonverbal Behavior, 13*, 67–82. https://doi.org/10.1007/BF00990791

Printed in the USA
CPSIA information can be obtained
at www.ICGtesting.com
LVHW061451221124
797189LV00008B/33